Growing Down

God's Grace, in Spite of Myself

Praise for *Growing Down*

We all learn from one another, and the learning makes an impact when the need goes beyond our attempts to figure out how to make life work. Sarah Wetzel weaves her own journey with what she learned from ten people from different walks of life, bringing her to a place of repentance and joy. I too have walked with some of the same people, especially my husband, Jack Miller. Learn from Sarah's life lessons; learn from the Spirit what it means to be *Growing Down*.

—Rose Marie Miller, missionary with World Harvest Mission; author, *From Fear to Freedom* and *Nothing Is Impossible With God*

I am grateful for this truth: "For my thoughts are not your thoughts, neither are your ways my ways, declares the Lord" (Isaiah 55:8). In *Growing Down*, Sarah Wetzel uses captivating stories—from personal experiences as a missionary, the biographies of others, and Bible studies—to reveal this reality, how God works in the hearts of his people. An informative and inspiring read.

—Bruce Johnson, president, SIM USA

Growing Down is about growing up in the joy of God's grace to us in Jesus. Sarah Wetzel has not written a how-to book on some ethereal victorious Christian life; She has given us an honest and vulnerable look at the "scum" in her heart that manifests in the everyday life issues of marriage, kids, and work. Looking through the lens of her own experience, along with that of other pilgrims on the journey ahead of her, and Scripture, Sarah delivers practical insights that will help any soul hungry for God understand what repentance looks like, with the encouragement that God means business in drawing us near and filling us with joy. Sarah's story is not only a great read for individuals; it would make an excellent small-group discussion book. I can't wait for it to be available to folks in our congregation, so they can begin thinking about growing down too.

—Richard White, senior pastor, Christ Community Church, Montreat, NC

As a former missionary who lived in Thailand for twenty-two years, my heart echoed, "Indeed!" so often as I read *Growing Down: God's Grace, in Spite of Myself.* Sarah Wetzel has identified the core struggle of so many who serve overseas—that of learning to trust the God we claim to be serving. This book challenges readers to ponder the paradox of suffering comingled with joy as a way of "growing down" into relationship with Christ. Wetzel's honest reflections about her own reluctant journey toward trusting God, and the surprise of finding his grace along the way, make this book a delightful read!

—Pamela S. Davis, PhD, assistant professor of psychology,
Wheaton College, IL

Sarah's remarkable life as a missionary, wife, and mother is a huge inspiration to today's Christian women who feel God's call to serve. This book is filled with refreshing, uncommon candor. A powerful and inspiring story.

—Lorraine Mazza, managing director of development, Joni and Friends
International Disability Center

Growing Down

God's Grace, in Spite of Myself

SARAH HORNER WETZEL

Deep River
B O O K S

ISBN – 13: 9781937756963
ISBN – 10: 1937756963

Library of Congress: 2013947805

Cover design by Connie Gabbert

Printed in the USA

To my dear dad,
Andy Horner,
whose happy humility is a benediction
to everyone who knows him.

And to my husband,
Jake,
who, like Jesus,
always has grace for me.

Contents

Foreword
~
Before You Begin . . .

I was fourteen years old, a babe in Christ, and excited about growing closer to God. As I scoured my brand-new Bible to find a verse that captured my fresh enthusiasm, I stumbled upon Philippians 3:8-9. It immediately resonated, so I reached for my yellow highlighter and illumined the words "I want to know Christ, and the power of his resurrection, and the fellowship of sharing in his sufferings, becoming like him in his death." Satisfied, I sat back and read it a second time: "I want to know Christ." *Yep, that's me. I definitely want to know Jesus better.*

" . . . and the power of his resurrection." *Power? Who doesn't want more power in their lives?! This is what the Christian life is all about, right? So bring it on!*

" . . . and the fellowship of sharing in his sufferings." *Hmm. Not too sure about this one. Then again, perhaps my soul does need a good scrubbing now and then, as long as the trials aren't too severe or inconvenient.*

" . . . becoming like him in his death." Such strange words made me wince. I totally did *not* get this one. *Maybe I can un-yellow-highlight this part,* I thought. And for all intents and purposes, I did. I memorized most of the verse but, over time, forgot all about those awkward, enigmatic last words.

I forgot, that is, until I broke my neck in a diving accident a few years

11

later. Quadriplegia was everything I dreaded: a trial way too severe and far too inconvenient. My paralysis was not merely a soul-scrubbing; it was a full-force sandblasting. And I was bristling with questions. Finally, when I was strong enough to sit up in a wheelchair, I positioned myself in front of a music stand that held books and my Bible. I was on a desperate search to understand what God was doing—why he allowed my accident to happen.

Using a mouth stick, I flipped furiously through the pages of my Bible. This time I wasn't looking for something that simply resonated or buzzed. I was searching for meaning, real and deep. Oddly, I kept coming across Philippians 3:8-9, the portion I memorized when the Christian life seemed easier. Somehow, I instinctively knew it held the key to my happiness—it had something to do with the fellowship of sharing in Christ's sufferings and becoming like him in his death. But what did it *mean*?

One day, my sister plopped on the music stand a book called *Valley of Vision*. It was a collection of Puritan prayers. One prayer especially caught my eye:

> Lord, let me learn by paradox that the way down is the way up, that to be low is to be high, that the broken heart is the healed heart, that the contrite spirit is the rejoicing spirit, that the repenting soul is the victorious soul, that to have nothing is to possess all, that to bear the cross is to wear the crown, that to give is to receive, that the valley is the place of vision. Lord, in the daytime stars can be seen from deepest wells, and the deeper the wells the brighter thy stars shine; Let me find thy light in my darkness, thy life in my death, thy joy in my sorrow, thy grace in my sin, thy riches in my poverty, thy glory in my valley.[1]

It was an aha moment, like God striking a match in my heart. I realized that to "become like Christ in his death" was the key to living— *really* living. The way down was my way up. To lower myself was to be lifted high. It wouldn't be easy, but from that day forward, I decided to "grow down," as the title of this book suggests. I turned my back on self-pity, fears, and most of all, my pride that secretly bristled against God.

Before long, the Lord opened his floodgate of grace and mercy, pouring out on me joy, peace, patience, and more perseverance than I ever dreamed possible. I had nothing, but possessed everything. I was still sorrowful, but rejoicing. I was completely paralyzed, but walking with the Lord like I had never experienced before!

The principles embraced in that *Valley of Vision* prayer are common throughout the Bible. We are all richer when we recognize our spiritual poverty. We are wiser when we acknowledge our foolishness. We are stronger when we admit our weaknesses. And the good news is, you don't have to experience the cross of quadriplegia to wear the crown of Christ in all its grace and glory.

It's why my friend Sarah Horner Wetzel wrote *Growing Down*. Sarah has traveled a different road than I have, but not *that* different. We both have faced life situations we never would have asked for, never would have chosen. But our deep disappointments and darkness drove us utterly to the end of ourselves—and Sarah and I both discovered that's not a bad place to be.

This is why her story is so much like yours. God would have us *all* find his light in our darkness, his joy in our sorrow, and the grace of Jesus in our sin. Sarah's is a simple, straightforward, and uncluttered story, a touching example of James 4:10: "When you bow down before the Lord and admit your dependence on him, he will lift you up and give you honor" (NLT).

It's something God challenges us all to do—to bow down before him and admit our dependence, our very desperate need of him. And the book you hold in your hands will help you do just that. Beginning with the title. For if you want to grow up in Christ, start by growing down. Uncertain how to do it? Well, let the journey begin by turning the page.

Joni Eareckson Tada

Introduction

We were staying in a quaint guesthouse on a quiet backstreet in bustling Nairobi, Kenya. My husband, Jake, and I had attended an African Christian camping conference, and now we had one free day before going on an animal safari. Usually I relish traveling and visiting new places, but that day I was in a funk. I didn't care about seeing the exotic sights of the city, I didn't want to go on the safari, and I was dreading the return to our then-difficult life in Ethiopia. I don't remember what Jake did that day, but I decided to do exactly what I felt like doing: nothing. I would stay at the guesthouse to rest, and my familiar friend, Self-Pity, would stay with me.

Going back to our room after breakfast, I passed a small library. Each wall was crowded with shelves, and each shelf sagged with dusty books. I love books. There was no way I could walk past that literary museum without taking time to admire its dingy treasures. I went in, and soon my head was cocking this way and that, my eyes scrambling to read the names in the piles and rows of books, until the title *Karen! Karen!* stopped me. I pulled the thin book from where it was jammed, and for the next few hours, it was as if author Karen Mains sat on my bed with me, telling me her stories.

Through that book, God intruded into my funk, calling my name, "Sarah! Sarah!" He invited me—again—to acknowledge my fears, and he reminded me—again—that he had a special purpose for my life. I repented of my resistance and surrendered—again—to his will. By suppertime, I felt new, inside and out, and ready to pack for the safari. For three days, on that vast Kenyan plain, I worshipped God. And I returned to my life in Ethiopia, praising him.

Throughout my life, this has happened many times: God uses a person through their book to interrupt my life story, to challenge my thinking, to show me my sin. Why does he do that? Does he want me to live in misery? Does he like discouraging me? Quite the opposite. God wants to free me and give me joy. I like the way J. I. Packer explains it:

> Watching your children grow up is, after all, an exciting business
> .... But growing *down* is something that every Christian must
> learn to do .... We grow *up* into Christ by growing *down* into
> lowliness (humility, from the Latin word *humilus*, meaning low).
> Christians, we might say, grow greater by getting smaller.
>
> Pride blows us up like balloons, but grace punctures our
> conceit and lets the hot, proud air out of our system. The result
> is that we shrink, and end up seeing ourselves as less—less nice,
> less able, less wise, less good, less strong, less steady, less com-
> mitted, less of a piece—than ever we thought we were. We stop
> kidding ourselves that we are persons of great importance to the
> world and to God. ... We give up our dreams of being greatly
> admired for doing wonderfully well.[1]

This is the work of God: To help me give up my dream of being admired by others; to convince me that, yes, I am "less of a piece" than I realize. He wants me to see the truth about myself, not to depress me, only to show me the truth about Jesus. Little by little, I am growing down.

This book is a collection of my humbling, grace-puncturing stories. You will meet some unique biblical characters, along with ten of my

God-sent "friends": Isobel Kuhn, Keith Green, Dr. John (Jack) Miller, Joni Eareckson Tada, Roy Hession, Dr. Kenneth Moynagh, Steve and Rujon Morrison, Sarah Young, Atticus Finch, and Catherine Marshall—friends who, by opening the door of their lives through their books, beckoned me to live in deeper grace and greater joy.

Now my door is open to you, dear reader. Come on in.

1
~

A Yearning

*Do not fancy that you are walking the path to holiness
if rebuke and repentance have no place in your life.*
—J. I. PACKER, *Rediscovering Holiness:
Know the Fullness of Life with God*

"So I quickly stomped my foot on the snake's neck..." The missionary speaker smashed his sandaled foot onto the hollow podium floor with a loud *thump*. "... and I pressed down hard while I finished preaching."

Wide-eyed boys and girls, crowded on the old wooden benches, stopped squirming and leaned forward to listen.

"Then a young man came up and killed it with a machete," he continued. "After that, we slid down the mud of that steep riverbank, packed our things onto the boat, then floated downriver to the next village, thanking God for his protection and for the new converts we had made. And now, campers, if you wanna see a real snake skin, like the big one that came to the jungle meeting that day, come to my table at the back."

I was one of those camper kids who rushed to examine the snake skin.

My first impressions of missionaries were formed at those hot, dusty, Texas summer church camps. Foreign relics and costumes captivated me, as did the miracle stories of God's care in dangerous places and his power to change lives. I wanted that kind of life; I wanted to live in a foreign country, experience God-stories and grow brave and spiritually strong. When I was around twelve years old, I stood up at the end of one of those services in the old open-air tabernacle, spontaneously responding to a preacher's mission challenge. From then on, I expected I'd become a missionary.

Ever since I can remember choosing my own books in the elementary school library, I preferred nonfiction—true stories of real life. I read a lot of biographies, especially about missionaries. As a child, I never questioned the lopsidedly heroic accounts, but as I became more aware of my own faults and weaknesses, I grew impatient with missionary stories that reported only the positive qualities of the person. That's why I was first attracted to Isobel Kuhn when I "met" her through her writing. In her autobiography, *In the Arena*, she wrote about the trials of her life with unfashionable openness and honesty.

Isobel Kuhn (1901–1957) grew up in a Christian home in Canada, but while at the University of British Columbia in Vancouver, after being ridiculed for believing in the biblical view of creation, she declared herself agnostic. She had a vivacious personality, and for the next few years, she determined to enjoy the world. Dancing, theater, friends, and parties filled her days. Isobel was talented, intelligent, and popular. But when the man she planned to marry ended their relationship abruptly, Isobel recognized that the world could not bring her joy, and she fell into despair.[1]

In her first book, *By Searching*, Isobel described the night she was planning to drink poison and die. That very night, a quote by Dante from her poetry study came into her mind: *In la sua volontade e nostra pace.* Isobel knew what it meant in Latin: "In His will is our peace." She didn't know if there was a God, but she turned her palms toward heaven and whispered, "God, if there be a God, if You will prove to me that You are, if You will give me peace, I will give You my whole life. I will do anything You ask me to do, go where You send me, obey You all my days."[2]

Then she fell fast asleep.The next morning, Isobel writes, she awoke, thinking, "Such deep relaxed slumber had not touched my pillow for many a long day. What had brought it?" Then she remembered. "I had made a bargain with God. I asked Him for peace and *peace had come*."[3] From that day on, Isobel searched diligently for God. She listened to Bible teachers and pastors and studied about Jesus. She became convinced that Jesus was God's Son, and she determined to follow him.

Isobel attended a missionary conference at The Firs, in Bellingham, Washington. When she heard about the needs of the Lisu people in China, her heart responded. Even though she was not a man—the speaker was urging men to go—she knew God was directing her. But when she told her parents of her desire to go to China, they opposed her.

"Over my dead body!" cried her mother. "I will never consent."[4] Formerly the president of the Women's Missionary Society, her mother was, of course, not against missions *in theory*. But she was completely against her only daughter going overseas. Isobel's parents had given her the finest education and comforts of life, so they viewed her plan as selfish and ungrateful. For several years, they tried to force their will on her, but Isobel was resolute; she continued to follow what she knew God was calling her to do. Isobel's mother died an early death, but not before she expressed a change of heart. In a letter to a friend, she wrote "I have come to the conclusion that all my busy Women's Missionary Society work has been but wood, hay, and stubble. I feel my little girl has chosen the better part in wishing to devote all her life to the Lord."[5]

Isobel moved to Chicago to study at Moody Bible Institute. There, a young man named John Kuhn caught her eye. Though opposites in many ways—Isobel was passionate and impulsive, while John was reserved and full of common sense—they shared the same yearning love for China.

My impressions of missionaries that began at church camp morphed and broadened during my four years at Wheaton College in Illinois. Besides the many missionaries I "knew" through books, like Isobel Kuhn, I met alumni from all parts of the world, hearing them speak and teach in chapel and workshops. I loved hanging out with real live "MKs" (missionary kids), eating curry and rice with a guy friend whose parents were doctors in India, sitting in class with a girlfriend who told me stories about her childhood in the Philippines, and leafing through the scrapbooks of my across-the-hall neighbor who grew up in Brazil. Overseas missionary life seemed to be a radical life of faith and adventure, with a real connection to Jesus and his love for the world. I yearned for that kind of life. Sometimes I would sit under an old oak tree on front campus and daydream. *Did I love the world like God did? Was he calling me to be a missionary?* I didn't know.

Curious to know if I had what it took, I applied for a summer student mission assignment during my second year at Wheaton. I was surprised to be rejected. "Try again for next summer," the letter read. So I did. I went through the application and interview processes again the next year, and I waited anxiously for my acceptance and details of my post. *What country would I be working in? What job would I be doing?*

But I was rejected again. I grieved and fumed and made an appointment with the dean of students. "What's wrong with me?" I insisted to know. He looked into my file and, in a kind, fatherly way, told me that the committee thought I would not be submissive to those in authority over me because I had been resistant to their rules. As his words sunk in, my lips clenched, and I left his quiet office with loud churning in my spirit. I wanted to argue and defend myself, but I knew it was true. My noncompliant nature was obvious; I had publicly disagreed with some of the unfair-in-my-eyes summer missions department's policies. But did that mean I wouldn't make a good short-term missionary? It was a hard blow.

Isobel Kuhn knew about rejection. Someone wrote a reference for her, calling her proud, disobedient, and likely to be a trouble maker. It kept her from being accepted by the China Inland Mission for several years. In Isobel's case, the reference was untrue and undeserved; she later found out that the source was a disgruntled, envious fellow teacher, but Isobel had already accepted the delay as part of God's good plan.

Indeed, God had good things planned for me as well for those two summers. In 1972, I jumped at the chance to study for two months in Israel. That was an awesome experience. Then, the second summer, I took a job doing maintenance and housekeeping at a camp in northern Wisconsin where, through the dirty-dish window, I first saw Jake Wetzel, the ruggedly handsome wilderness leader who would become my husband six months later.

But I continued to nurse the painful wound of rejection. My heart was set on becoming a missionary, so I convinced Jake to apply with me to be houseparents for an orphanage in Ireland. *Maybe they will consider me fit to be a missionary now that I'm married*, I thought.

That rejection letter arrived in record time: *We do not accept newlyweds. Please submit your application again next year.* I'd heard that "next year" idea before. That was my third strike and I knew I was out. We did not reapply. I resigned myself to the reality that I was not going to be a missionary.

The first year of our marriage was difficult for me, working in the camp kitchen while Jake led wilderness trips and outdoor programs. So when Jake was hired to start a wilderness program at Montreat College in the Blue Ridge Mountains of North Carolina, I was more than thrilled. Two months after our first anniversary, we stuffed our red VW van with our belongings and drove south to our new home: three dorm rooms on the first hall of a big stone building where Jake was the residence director. We enjoyed living on campus, working with student leaders, developing Jake's outdoor skills classes and running a small summer camp for local children.

Eventually we bought an old tumbly house with a big front porch next to a loud rocky creek and settled down, collecting daughters and friends and happy memories. I didn't know it then, of course, but God was building a base camp for our family, a place in the community of Montreat where we would return throughout all our future comings and goings.

Eight years went by. Jake thought he had the best job in the world, and I was loving small-town life. But curiously, there came a time when we both felt unsatisfied; we shared an odd restlessness. We thought maybe we should look into full-time camp ministry, so we began exploring possibilities in Texas and Colorado. Funny, I never imagined that God was at work, fulfilling my dream. Then one hot, muggy day in the summer of 1982, a representative from the Sudan Interior Mission organization dropped by for a spontaneous visit.

Based in Charlotte, SIM is one of the oldest international missions organizations, with hundreds of missionaries serving all over the world. He had our address because we sent a few dollars each month to a missionary family in Liberia. Jake was not home at the beginning of his visit, and the girls were napping, so I poured out my long story of rejections to the pleasant old gentleman. "I still want to be a missionary," I told him, "but my husband teaches rock climbing and canoeing, and he doesn't think he has any skills to offer on the mission field."

After Jake got home and joined the conversation, the man from SIM encouraged us to send his little postcard to the mission headquarters, to see if there were any camp job openings overseas. Jake was hesitant, but the next day I mailed it, and soon afterward we received a letter describing a children's camp on the beach of Liberia, West Africa that needed a director for two years. They invited Jake to apply for the position.

Step by step, we moved forward. Doctrinal papers, psychological tests, and interviews—we made it through all the requirements and were accepted. I was beginning to believe that, yes, God *had* put this yearning in my heart; he had been calling me all along.

Now Jake and I are not beach people. The seashore is a beautiful place to vacation, but we'd choose to live in cool mountain air rather than in a hot and humid climate. But that year we primed ourselves to leave the mountains and live at the beach in Liberia. Jake was planning to get a sea kayak, and we were looking forward to being with children in that English-speaking country. Then, surprise! At our month-long candidate school, we heard about another camp needing a director, this one located in the Andes Mountains of Bolivia. It was a career position and included going to language school.

Viewing slides of the camp in Bolivia, we began to have second thoughts. The beautiful camp property by a cobalt-blue lake, surrounded by the greens and browns of patchwork farming on steep mountainsides, the handsome young people with their guitars, and the balanced pyramids of amazing fruits and vegetables at their outdoor markets: *Could God want us to go there? Could it possibly be his will for us to live in such a beautiful place?* A director was needed at both camps, and the mission gave us complete freedom to choose. It was a puzzling time for us, looking at all the pieces, trying to discern God's will between Africa and South America. But at the end of those two weeks, Jake and I fully agreed: we would take the deeper plunge, the longer road, and go to Bolivia.

Finally the day came. After ten years of marriage and with our three small daughters, five-year-old Johannah, three-year-old Miah, and eight-month-old Gabrielle (Caris, our fourth, was born three years later), Jake and I boarded a plane in Miami in the middle of the night, bound for Cochabamba, Bolivia. My life dream to be a missionary was beginning!

John Kuhn left for China with the China Inland Mission (CIM) in 1926, and two years later, Isobel followed him. There, they wed. Isobel candidly described those first years in China as uncomfortable. Unaccustomed to the diet, the customs, the lack of personal space, and adjusting to married life, Isobel paid the high cost of leaving home, and she struggled with all the changes. She thrilled at sharing God's love with visitors in her home, but sat aghast when one of the Chinese women blew her nose onto her special quilt, while another allowed her child to spit up all over Isobel's pretty rug.

On the boat trip over, an experienced missionary informed the new recruits that in China, all the "scum" in their hearts would be exposed. Isobel wrote in *In the Arena*:

> All of us were nice girls, were we not? Scum? And so I was totally unprepared for the revolt of the flesh that was waiting for me on China's shores. The day was to come when on my knees in the Lord's presence I had to say, "Lord, *scum* is the only word to describe me."[6]
> . . . I have never attained the place where one is beyond the temptations of self. But I want to testify to what God can do to change a human being, one that found she was indeed—scum.[7]

Isobel recorded many miracles and special blessings, but she never wanted anyone to read about the favor God showed her and think it was because she was a wonderful Christian, worthy of such blessing. To make her point, she wrote about the Old Testament King David and Ahithophel. David and Ahithophel were at one time close friends; Ahithophel was one of David's principal advisors. Ahithophel's granddaughter was Bathsheba, so he knew all too well the details and repercussions of David's horrible sins: adultery with Bathsheba and the murder of her husband (see 2 Samuel 11).

When David was confronted by the prophet Nathan, he confessed his sin and was restored to God (2 Samuel 12). But Ahithophel? He refused to accept that God granted forgiveness and grace to David. His heart became hard with anger, and he switched his loyalties and counsel to David's son Absalom—who was opposing his father, King David. Ahithophel, who had once hated David's sin of adultery, advised Absalom to do the same—commit sexual sin. And he who criticized David for murder took his own life in the end (2 Samuel 16:20; 17:23).

Isobel pointed out that if Ahithophel had seen his need for God's grace and repented of his proud heart, perhaps he would have lived to celebrate the crowning of his great-grandson Solomon as king. "God blessed the sinner who opened his heart to correction," she observed, "and God's blessing was lost to the sinner who closed his heart to the pleadings of grace and refused to forgive. We do not receive His blessings then because we deserve them, but only when we obey His tender injunction, 'Open thy mouth wide and I will fill it.' I have had a greedily wide mouth, but if it had been wider, I might have received more."[8]

Isobel Kuhn lived in China and Thailand for almost twenty years. She served and taught the Lisu people with enthusiasm, commitment, and love. At the height of her ministry, she was diagnosed with aggressive cancer; she died at the age of fifty-six. *In the Arena* was written during those last years of her life. Isobel Kuhn wrote openly about how God used her trials and struggles, her humanness and her repentances, to give her joy and peace and to show others God's great grace, blessing, and power.

Jake and I never regretted our choice to move to South America, and for twenty-one years God gave us many blessings. We grew accustomed to the relaxed culture, learned the Spanish language, and fell in love with the warm, humble Bolivian people. Johannah, Miah, Gaby, and Caris were educated at the international mission school in the city where we lived and they fancied being the camp director's daughters, working at camp peeling potatoes in the kitchen, selling (and eating!) candy and fried egg sandwiches in the camp store, helping with crafts and games, and sometimes being campers themselves. Our family thrived in Bolivia.

The Lord blessed others as well. Through Jake's leadership, the camp property at 10,000 feet in the Andes Mountains was renovated and remodeled, young people were trained in camp work, and a year-round program was developed. With the dedicated team of leaders, who became like family to us and to our girls, we organized camps for thousands of city and rural children and young people to come and have fun and learn about Jesus. How satisfying it was to know we were doing work that made an eternal difference in people's lives!

But at the same time, something inside of me began to unravel. Like he did for Isobel Kuhn, God wanted to expose the scum hiding in my heart.

2
~

A Disconnect

All human nature vigorously resists grace because grace changes us and the change is painful.
—FLANNERY O'CONNOR, *The Habit of Being: Letters of Flannery O'Connor*

It was the summer of 1982. My sister was sobbing on the phone. "Sarah, have you heard? Keith Green was killed in a small plane crash. And he was only twenty-eight years old!"

I had heard of Keith Green; I knew he was a popular Christian singer-songwriter, but I didn't share my sister's sorrow. At the time, I never imagined that nine years later God would use Keith's life story to disturb mine.

Jake and I were living in Cochabamba, Bolivia, doing youth and camp work. Outwardly everything seemed fine and flourishing. Jake had plenty of good work to do, both at the camp property, a one-and-a half hour commute from our house, and at the camp office in the city: overseeing building projects, planning programs, finding and training staff, and buying bushels and gallons of food for the camps. Our girls were at the fun ages of three, six, nine, and eleven, and I loved being their mom. I kept busy in our home, making menus and market trips, cooking, and keeping the floors and dishes and clothes washed and dried. It was a lot of work! I was grateful for our big washing machine and for Cati, who helped me with all the daily chores.

As I said, outwardly everything appeared hunky-dory. But it wasn't.

In January 1991, I was flipping through old entries in my journal, as was my custom at the beginning of each new year. That time it struck me that something was wrong. Each January, I would choose one fruit of the Spirit from the apostle Paul's list in Galatians—"The fruit of the Spirit is love, joy, peace, patience, kindness, goodness, faithfulness, gentleness, self-control" (Galatians 5:22–23)—and I would focus on that attribute all year long, trying to change my character. My plan was not working.

Where was the love, joy, peace, and gentleness? Instead, I was tired of all the poverty and street beggars, I criticized fellow missionaries who were different from me, and many days at home there were those "witch hours": the late afternoon until the girls' bedtime, when I felt like a "witch"—unkind, harsh, and ugly—the exact opposite of what I longed to be. And I seemed to be getting worse rather than better. *I must be crazy to think I could become like Christ.*

Something else bothered me. Not one person I knew of had decided to follow Jesus because of *my* witness. No one in my entire life—and I was a missionary! Wasn't it my *job* to lead others to Christ? The previous January, I had specifically prayed, "Lord, give me just one soul this year. One convert. Just one." God had denied my fervent request. That, along with seeing no positive changes in my heart or behaviors discouraged me, and I became angry. *What's going on? What's wrong with God? Why hasn't he changed me? Why isn't he using me?*

That was the very month I spied Keith Green's biography, *No Compromise,* on a bookshelf in the sitting room of our missionary guesthouse. I picked it up, not knowing that God had a life-changing message in store for me through Keith's story.

Keith Green was born in New York City, but his family moved to Hollywood when he was very young. By the age of two, he had surprised his parents with his singing ability. Keith could remember melodies with perfect pitch, and he was writing his own songs on the piano before he was six years old.

At eleven, Keith signed a recording contract with a major music company and was on his way toward his dream of being a pop star. But teen star Donny Osmond came on the scene at the same time, and Keith's hope for fame was frustrated. When he was fifteen, he ran away from home, looking for adventure in music and the free-love movement of the 1960s. At nineteen, he met his match in Melody, another hippie-like musician and spiritual seeker, and together they chased happiness and musical fame.

Although Keith was raised a Christian Scientist and had grown up reading the Bible, he rejected the fundamental Christian belief that the whole Bible is God's word. He didn't like the idea that even though God created us, we are sinners and therefore blocked from having a relationship with him. Keith believed he could connect with God on his own, and he experimented with different religions, philosophies, and spiritual exercises. He tried Flower Power, Buddhism, Mother Nature, the occult, LSD, mescaline, and mysticism. He had his tarot cards read and followed astrology charts. Everything left him disillusioned.

Keith felt a sense of calling on his life, a spiritual destiny he was serious about finding. He was looking for something worth living for. After a particularly frightening drug trip, he doubted everything and everybody, so he stopped all spiritual exercises, except for reading the Christian Science literature and the Bible. His biographers, Melody Green and David Hazard, write:

> There seemed to be one common thread running through all the teachings that Keith studied. That thread was Jesus Christ. Everybody seemed to say that, at the very least, Jesus was a "good guy." Some said he was the Son of God, others said he was a prophet; others said he was an ascended spiritual master—even Buddha

thought he was okay. And to top it off, Jesus even said good things about himself. Jesus said he was the only way to God.[1]

Keith made Jesus his spiritual guru. He bought an old, worn crucifix necklace at a secondhand shop. As he drove away, with the cross around his neck, he began to pray "to a God he did not know":

It wasn't a tidy little religious prayer. It was rough and uneven, a prayer of desperation. Keith knew he'd reached the bottom of his list. Everything was scratched off but Jesus. If Jesus didn't come through he didn't know what he'd do. But before he could get any words out, gathering tears started spilling down his cheeks and running into his beard. In between broken sobs, he choked out a prayer: "Jesus, oh, Jesus, . . . if you are really real. If you are who you say you are, please prove it to me. I need you. I need something. . . . Show me the way and I'll serve you forever."[2]

God heard his prayer. It would take some years before Keith accepted all of Jesus' words in the Bible and understood about Christ's redemptive death on the cross for his sin. But that day he put his trust in Jesus, and as he turned from his sins, Keith experienced true peace and power from God. Over time, he and Melody kicked the drugs, and they never stopped talking about Jesus and what he had done for them. They helped anyone in their circle of friends—the homeless, the poor, and the addicted. Anyone searching for God was welcomed to live with them in their home.

Keith's passionate songs told about his joy in the forgiveness of sin and about following Jesus. He denounced sin, publicly pointing a finger at his own laziness, impatience, pride, and cold heart. He was unashamed of the Good News of the Bible—the gospel[3]—and he repeatedly confessed his sins with tears of repentance, rejoicing in God's forgiveness with tears of jubilation. Through packed concerts and individual conversations, he begged others to wake up, see their need, and turn to God.

Reading Keith's story while in Bolivia made me doubt the reality of my relationship with God. Had I ever truly repented? I couldn't remember weeping over my sins. I felt embarrassed or ashamed when I did wrong, but sorrow toward God? That was foreign to me. Where was my love for God and for lost, hurting people? I had neither passion nor compassion to tell others about Jesus. And joy? Where was the joy Keith had when he prayed and read the Bible? Why was I not more like Keith?

Then one Sunday morning in our little Bolivian church around the corner from our home, sitting on the wooden pew with my family, I was thinking about a man who wasn't my husband. I'd had a long conversation with him the day before, I'd been enjoying his company and attention, but he had left on a trip and I was missing him. A voice broke into my daydreams with a piercing question: "Sarah, what are you doing?"

What *was* I doing? I was thinking about a single man, a guy I had been adjusting my life to be around for several months, trying to get to know him, trying to impress him. It wasn't physical, but I knew that in God's eyes a woman seeking emotional connection with a man other than her husband was as serious as committing adultery. Sitting in church, no one had a clue my soul had been stabbed by a divine knife. I was horrified at the thought of what *might* have happened—I could have lost and ruined my family.

That very minute, I vowed to avoid the man, who had no idea of my feelings. And that afternoon, I wrote a letter to an older friend, in order to be accountable to someone. I also confessed to Jake. It sickens me to remember how I told him, how I wrongly blamed him for *my* sinful actions. And I also blamed God, for not keeping me from this temptation and sin. *God, why did you let me feel attracted to that man? What else am I blind to?* A black cloud rolled in between me and God.

Saul of the Old Testament had something like a black cloud between him and God also (1 Samuel 10–18). His story is a sad one. When God chose young Saul to be king of Israel, the Bible says the Spirit of God rushed upon him, he was "turned into another man," and "God gave him another heart" (1 Samuel 10:6,9). Saul belonged to God. But later, he was rejected by God and evil spirits used by God began to haunt him (1 Samuel 16:14-23). So what happened?

The first recorded story about Saul after he was confirmed as king is a war story. Saul commanded the Israelite army against the Philistines. First Samuel 13:5 records that the Philistines had "thirty thousand chariots, six thousand horsemen and troops like the sand on the seashore." When the Israelites saw their enemies mobilized for an attack, they panicked and "hid themselves in holes and in rocks and in tombs and in cisterns." The men who stayed with Saul were petrified with fear.

Saul waited for the prophet-priest Samuel to come and invoke God's help for the battle. When Samuel did not appear after seven days and the last of his frightened men began to flee, Saul called for the sacrificial animals and made the burnt offerings himself—something only a priest was permitted to do. Just as Saul finished, Samuel arrived, and he must have smelled the smoking altar because when Saul greeted him, Samuel rebuked him with a question: "What have you done?" (v. 10).

Saul tried to explain his predicament and how the pressing circumstances had compelled him. But he had broken God's commandments, as well as Samuel's specific instructions: "Seven days you shall wait until I come to you and show you what you shall do" (1 Samuel 10:8). Samuel's strong prophecy proclaimed the seriousness of Saul's sin: "You have done foolishly. . . . But now your kingdom shall not continue. The Lord has sought out a man after his own heart. . . . to be prince over his people, because you have not kept the Lord's command" (1 Samuel 13:13–14).

Following the battle with the Amalekites, King Saul blatantly disobeyed God a second time. He spared the life of Agag, the Amalekite
king, and kept the best of the animals—even though God had told him
to kill everything. When Samuel confronted Saul that time, he lied,
never mentioning the captive king, and he blamed his soldiers, saying,
"They spared the best of the sheep and cattle to sacrifice to the Lord your
God, but we totally destroyed the rest" (1 Samuel 15:15). Samuel reacted
fiercely. "Stop! Let me tell you what the Lord said to me last night." The
Lord's words were strong against Saul's rebellion, arrogance, and rejection of God's word.

And Saul's response? "I have sinned," he said. "I violated the Lord's
commands and your instructions. I was afraid of the people and so I gave
in to them. Now I beg you, forgive my sin and come back with me, so that
I may worship the Lord" (vv. 24–25).

That sounds good. It seems like Saul repented of his sin, asked for
forgiveness, and wanted to worship God. But look at Samuel's response:
"I will not go back with you. You have rejected the word of the Lord, and
the Lord has rejected you" (v. 26). Saul dramatically grabbed Samuel's
robe and pleaded with him, but Samuel pulled away and, as his robe
ripped, said to Saul, "The Lord has torn the kingdom of Israel from you
today." Saul's disobedience revealed his arrogant, independent heart and
his demanding words exposed his pride and lack of repentance. The last
verse of 1 Samuel 15 says, "Until the day Samuel died, he did not go to see
Saul again, though Samuel mourned for him." Saul forfeited his relationship with Samuel and with God because he would not humble himself.
How tragic.

Remember Samuel's words in 1 Samuel 13:14? He said because of Saul's
foolish actions, the Lord was sorry he had made Saul king and he would look
for "a man after his own heart." God led Samuel to the home of Jesse, where he
was very impressed with Jesse's eldest son. But he heard the Lord say, "Do not
look on his appearance or on the height of his stature, because I have rejected
him. For the Lord sees not as man sees. Man looks on the outward appearance,

but the Lord looks on the heart" (1 Samuel 16:7). Seven brothers, one by one, stood before Samuel, until the youngest son of Jesse came in. "Arise and anoint him; for this is he," the Lord said (v. 12). That young man was David.

The Lord knew the wrongs David would commit, how he would lie, disobey, commit adultery, and even murder an innocent man. But God saw David's heart. God knew that David would always return to him. Saul's sins—rebellion, arrogance, rejection of God's word—those deep heart sins, were not in David.

When Saul defended himself, he said they had spared the best animals to sacrifice "to the Lord *your* God" (1 Samuel 15:21, italics mine). Whereas David, as we see in the Psalms, which he wrote throughout his life, consistently and repeatedly spoke of God as "*my* God": "O God, you are *my* God; earnestly I seek you" (Psalm 63:1, italics mine). "The Lord is *my* shepherd" (Psalm 23, italics mine). "You are *my* God, and I will give thanks to you" (Psalm 118:28, italics mine). David was closely connected with God.

In my mind, Keith Green was a lot like King David. Not only were they both poets and songwriters, but also both related to God in a deep-heart way. Both wept over their sins. Both sang and danced with joy.

David's public and private sins are recorded in the Bible. In fact, David focused much of his own writing on God's great mercy, forgiveness, and cleansing because of his own experience and need. It is the theme of Psalm 51, which David recorded after confessing his adultery with Bathsheba:

> Have mercy on me, O God, according to your steadfast love; according to your abundant mercy blot out my transgressions. Wash me thoroughly . . . and cleanse me from my sin! For . . . my sin is ever before me. Against you, you only, have I sinned and done what is evil in your sight. . . . Purge me with

hyssop, and I shall be clean; wash me, and I shall be whiter than snow. Let me hear joy and gladness; let the bones that you have broken rejoice. (Psalm 51: 1–4, 7–8)

Also in this psalm, David wrote the beautiful words that inspired one of Keith Green's signature songs:

Create in me a clean heart, O God, and renew a right spirit in me. Cast me not away from your presence, and take not your Holy Spirit from me. Restore to me the joy of your salvation and uphold me with a willing spirit. (Psalm 51:10–12)

Keith's desire for popularity and fame changed into a passion for Jesus. Within a few years after his conversion to Christ, thousands of people filled enormous stadiums to listen to Keith sing; his albums were on the top of the charts. He decided not to charge admission for his concerts and he gave away his music for free. During Keith's short life, his whole desire was to please God, to do whatever God told him with no compromise. He was radical and controversial. He was misunderstood and criticized. But he never stopped speaking boldly for God, never quit urging people to turn from their self-centered ways and believe in Jesus. Many years after his death, his life still speaks.

It spoke to me.

Keith Green's story illuminated some alarming truths about my own relationship with Jesus. I had called myself a Christian virtually all my life, yet never experienced sorrowful repentances and the resulting joy in God's forgiveness and grace like Keith Green experienced. I didn't love God intensely like he did. After reading his biography, I seriously wondered if I was even a Christian.

The black cloud grew bigger. As we prepared to return to the United States for a year's home assignment, I told Jake I could no longer be a missionary. Like Saul, I was disconnected from God.

3
~

A Humbling

Only those who face their sinfulness can relax in God's grace.
—JERRY BRIDGES, *Transforming Grace*

If someone could get to heaven and have joy on earth by being a serious Christian, surely I could. On almost the first Sunday of my existence, I was in the church pew—bundled in my mother's arms, of course—and so began my record of near-perfect attendance. Growing up, I rarely missed church activities: girls' clubs, summer camp, vacation Bible schools, choir tours. When I was seven, kneeling with my mother at our living room couch, I asked Jesus to come into my heart. At ten, in a small Baptist church, I was baptized. And as a twelve-year-old at summer camp, I stood to commit my life to God for full-time Christian service.

I attended a Christian college and majored in Christian education. I volunteered with an inner-city church during the school terms and at a Christian camp one summer, where I met my Christian husband. Together, we worked at a Christian college and after ten years of marriage, we moved to Bolivia as Christian missionaries, doing youth work at a Christian camp there. Anyone could plainly see that Sarah Wetzel was serious about being a Christian.

But at the end of our seventh year of missionary service, I was rudely awakened. While filling out our mission organization's evaluation forms, I could not ignore two facts: Number One, I had never led anyone to Christ; Number Two, I had no joy.

For years, I had worked to attain the "fruit of the Spirit" as described in Galatians 5: Love, joy, peace, patience, gentleness, kindness, faithfulness, self-control. Yet I saw no improvement. My best quality, seriousness, wasn't even on Paul's list! But what especially bothered me was my lack of real joy. And then there was the massive shock when God showed me my grave moral sin—desiring intimacy with a man other than my husband.

I felt disconnected from God, and I gave up trying to "do" the Christian life. More of my true self leaked out for all to see—impatience, criticalness, gossip. I recognized these bad habits, and discovered even more—bitterness, lack of love for others, a sense of entitlement, jealousy. My heart was full of wrong attitudes.

It was 1991. Our family settled into life in the States for one year of home assignment, the customary time for missionaries to visit those who support them financially and in prayer. Our four daughters were ages three through eleven, in four different schools. Schedules, carpools, meals, and housework overwhelmed me. I was collapsing under all the obligations of American life. My stomach churned, headaches dogged me, and I was discouraged and in a chronic bad mood. I resented anyone who needed something from me. I couldn't even give a smile freely.

I figured that since I could not do the Christian life, everyone else must be faking it, too. To my mind, it was impossible to live like Jesus, so all of Christianity must be a lie, a psychological crutch. I convinced Jake we were done with missionary work, and I wondered how and when we would tell our friends and supporters.

I had to blame the turmoil on something. It must be burnout. Or maybe "reverse culture shock"—what some missionaries experience when they return to their homeland after years away. Or was it because

I was turning forty, having a midlife crisis? Was it an early-menopausal, hormone-based emotional trip? I even wondered if my stomach pains might be caused by Bolivian amoebas in my gut, and whether my tortured brain was a symptom they'd spread upward. (It does happen!)

I wanted to become an agnostic. Maybe then I would find inner peace.

Isolated within my dark cloud, I gave a clear *no* to every invitation, especially to Bible studies. I could barely sit through Sunday morning services and I no longer believed in the power of prayer. I tried to avoid people, but I had a stubborn friend who insisted I go with her to a ladies' group at another church, a Bible study on the book of Galatians. Reluctantly, I consented. No one knew me in that group, so I felt free to be myself. I criticized the teaching and avoided making friends with the other twelve ladies. I disdained the prayer time, so when we went around the table sharing requests, I would snobbishly say, "Pass." Every Thursday, as I drove out of that church parking lot, I told myself, *I am not coming back. I do not like that guy.*

"That guy" was pastor-author Dr. C. John Miller, who everyone just called Jack. In his video lectures, he said things that stunned me and left me defensive. *I've been a Christian my whole life and I have never heard that!* What really bugged me was his cheerfulness. Jack Miller laughed too much and his happiness mocked my misery. How did he get that joy?

Jack Miller was Oregon-raised to be an autonomous, self-confident man. When he was a young man, while reading the first chapter of Ephesians, he realized how alienated he was from God. Jack described that day, saying, "Suddenly I knew a God of all grace and He changed me. I was filled with incredible joy."[1]

As the years went by, Jack received much Christian education and experience, and he was praised and affirmed by many, but his joy dissipated. He was leading a church in California when he realized something had gone awry. He told this story:

I was driving down the street, and I heard some noise from a drive-in restaurant. Here was a white-haired lady carrying a market basket down the street. Eight or ten boys were throwing stones at her and yelling at her. I couldn't believe my ears! Being a good Boy Scout from Oregon where we helped old ladies to cross streets, I was enraged. I had forgotten that for years I had been an atheist and a wild kid myself.[2]

Jack turned his car into the parking lot to confront the gang and then panicked. He had never done anything so bold before. But his annoyance was strong, and he went over to the boys and asked them if they had heard of the fifth commandment, to honor parents and one's elders. They said they never had, so Jack began to preach to them and invited them to church. He never expected they would go, but the leader actually did! Jack did not know what to do with him.

The experience showed Jack the hardness of his own heart, how he used the law to correct others while living isolated from God's grace himself. He lacked a sense of conviction about his own failures. As he put it, "I didn't say 'Fellas, I'm a lot like you. I used to be *just* like you.' I didn't do that kind of thing [throwing stones at old ladies], but I probably did things that were worse in God's eyes."[3]

Jack started asking himself the question the apostle Paul put to the Galatian church, "What has happened to all your joy?" (Galations 4:15). Jack knew that Paul was not writing about ordinary joy. He meant all the fullness of life that God wants to give, a joy that becomes strength that flows out of the truths of the gospel through God's Spirit. Jack had lost the power and joy and freedom he'd known at his conversion. He had drifted into living like a spiritual orphan—independent, alone, burdened with life's obligations, and powerless—not like a beloved son trusting the gracious heavenly Father.

Some years later, Jack moved his family to Pennsylvania where he pastored a church and taught at an evangelical seminary. In one of his lectures, he confessed that as he got older, he became more critical of people—better at "estimating character," as he put it. He began to disagree with his colleagues and, eventually, resigned from both the church and seminary "with a flourish." Everyone else seemed proud and weak, and Jack felt he was too good for them all.

But God opened his eyes, and he saw that he was the big sinner, even bigger than those he had judged. He was proud, cynical, and a gossip. Seeing the depth of his sin depressed him, so when his wife Rose Marie suggested they retreat in Spain, he agreed. For three months, Jack studied the promises of God every day, from Genesis through Revelation. God's word confronted and comforted him, and he came back to Pennsylvania a humbled, changed man. He retracted his resignations and resumed teaching with great zeal, out of God's deep love for sinners—and with a passion for the Cross and Jesus Christ.

It irked me, as I sat in the Bible study hearing Jack Miller say, "We have nothing to give to Jesus, except our sin." *What? Nothing?* I had given Jesus my life. Was he saying Jesus didn't want my life? All I had done and all I had sacrificed—wasn't it worth something in God's eyes? And if it was true, then why had I never heard it before? I became angrier, and my frustrations seeped out at every turn. I, who had never been around cursing, began to use cusswords, shocking even me.

One Thursday on my way to Bible study, I dropped off my three-year-old daughter at my friend Jessie's house. She was graciously keeping Caris every Thursday afternoon with her little daughter. Standing in the driveway, Jessie said something about enjoying getting to know me, because I "was nothing like what she had heard." That did it. I blew up in her face. I don't remember the words I said to her, but I drove off, puffed up with self-righteous anger, muttering, *"I hate this town! I hate Christians! Everybody gossips. Everyone is a hypocrite!"*

Driving down Interstate 40 en route to the church, I pulled out the memory verse card. I at least wanted to be able to recite the homework verse so I wouldn't embarrass myself. When I saw that it was Galatians 2:20, I smugly thought, *No problem. Already know that one.* But when I said Paul's words out loud, "I have been crucified with Christ," something stunned me inside, and I "heard" an offer, a question in my head: "Would you like this angry Sarah to die? She can die and I will live my life in you."

It was the best offer I'd ever heard.

Yes! Let her die! my thoughts cried. I had tried and tried to manage Sarah, to change her, to improve her, to make her into a spiritual giant. All in vain. But she could just die and start over? I continued saying the verse, claiming it for myself: "It is no longer I—the hypocritical Sarah— who live, but Christ who lives in me. And the life I now live in the flesh I live by faith in the Son of God, who loved me and gave himself for me." The dark cloud over me disappeared, and a shaft of sunshine-glory-warmth seemed to descend from the sky and fill my van. God's acceptance and love, his peace and joy surrounded me. The fall colors of the world brightened, the trees and mountains seemed to dance and sing along with my heart and soul. And I couldn't wipe the smile off my face.

When I walked into the Bible study classroom, the leader greeted me, saying, "What happened to *you*?"

"I think I just met Jesus," I told her. At my own church the next week, friends noticed my new smile and wanted to know what had changed. I didn't—and still don't—know how to explain the miracle. I did nothing to deserve it. I thank God for proving the reality of his grace and love to me that day on I-40.

From that day on, I drank in everything Jack Miller and his wife, Rose Marie, poured out in their lectures and writings. In his book *Repentance: A Daring Call to Real Surrender*, Jack could have been describing me when he wrote of being "someone who is secretly proud that he is a spiritual Christian of a special class. He no longer looks to Christ in love. Instead he mounts a pedestal and quenches the Holy Spirit by denying the reality of the sin which yet remains in him and which must be put to death by active reliance on Christ. . . . He can no longer freely admit that he must confess his pride and unbelief on a daily basis."[4]

I thought that others had hoisted me up onto that missionary pedestal, and I had been resenting them for it. Instead I learned that I am the one who climbed up there, and there was only one way to come down and stay down: confess my pride *every day* and rely on Christ *every day*. Jack's teaching on the truths of Galatians humbled me and brought me into fresh experiences of God's grace, over and over.

I am so glad Jack was right when he taught that the only thing I have to give to Jesus is my sin. By accepting the sin that was in me, naming it, and giving it to Jesus, I felt free.

Jack also liked to teach the story of Jesus and Simon the Pharisee found in Luke 7:36–50. Pharisees were the Jewish religious leaders of Jesus' day. They were highly respected by the Jewish populace and, out of jealousy, suspicious of Jesus. A Pharisee named Simon invited Jesus into his home, yet for some curious reason, he neglected the common courtesies and practices of hospitality that were customary in their culture. He gave Jesus no kiss of greeting and did not have a servant wash Jesus' feet. After inviting him into his home, why did he ignore and thus dishonor Jesus?

Once Jesus found his place at the table, a woman—a prostitute—came up behind him, holding a perfume flask and weeping. She bent down and let the water of her tears rinse off Jesus' dusty feet. Then she wiped them with her hair and anointed Jesus with a pungent, sweet, expensive fragrance. Her display of love for Jesus was daring, scandalous, and very public—a drama heard, seen, smelled, and discussed by everyone around that table and out on the street.

It was not just her bold actions they criticized, but also Jesus, for allowing himself to be touched in such an intimate way by an "unclean" woman.

Jesus knew what Simon was thinking: "If this man were a prophet, he would have known who and what sort of woman this is touching him—that she is a sinner" (v. 39).

Jesus confronted Simon's judgmental thoughts using a hypothetical story about two debtors. One man owed a moneylender the equivalent of wages for 500 days of work. The other man owed the equivalent of fifty days of work. The moneylender decided to cancel the debt of both men. Jesus asked Simon, "Which one of them will love him more?" (v. 42). Simon replied, "The one, I suppose, for whom he cancelled the larger debt" (v. 43). He *supposed*? Of course Simon knew the answer, but he resisted the implication.

Then Jesus explained clearly what he was teaching. He turned to the woman still at his feet, as he spoke to Simon, "Do you see this woman? I entered your house. You gave me no water for my feet, but she has wet my feet with her tears and wiped them with her hair. You gave me no kiss, but from the time I came in she has not ceased to kiss my feet. You did not anoint my head with oil, but she has anointed my feet. . . . Therefore I tell you, her sins, which are many, are forgiven—for she loved much. But he who is forgiven little, loves little" (Luke 7:44–47).

I wonder what Simon did next. I readily identify with him, for I am Pharisee-like in my heart. Pride, arrogance, seeking the approval of man, hypocrisy—I think highly of myself, and I judge others for their wrongs. But oh, how I want to be like that contrite, humble woman! She loved Jesus so much because she knew that, although her sins were many, he forgave her. He loved her. She knew the greatness of her sin; so, also she felt the greatness of God's grace and forgiveness. I began to pray the way Jack Miller modeled, asking God to show me my sin, help me to hate it, and believe in his great grace and love.

"Cheer up! You're worse than you think!" Jack would say, with his eyes sparkling. "We're here to encourage you. The best news that you have ever heard is that original sin is true. If original sin is true, then the grace is true and the gospel is the power of God. The gospel is preparing us for a life of challenge and dying and suffering. It's not only, 'Cheer up! You're worse than you think.' But 'Cheer up! Come and die!' It's a great way to find life."[5]

I thank God often for that day on Interstate 40 when I, so undeserving, received forgiveness and joy from him. I can see he put Jack Miller in my life to teach me how much God loves sinners and how to reconnect to God through his good gift of repentance.

And what about my one best quality, religious seriousness? Instead, I became serious about repentance and I experienced serious joy! I couldn't wait to get back to Bolivia to tell others about God's grace.

4

~

A Flourishing

*To move forward on the road to holiness means
to know Jesus better. The better we come to know him,
the more plainly we shall see how little like him we are.*
—STEPHEN NEILL, *Christian Holiness*

By the time our family returned to Bolivia after our furlough year in 1992, I felt like a different person. I was living in the spacious freedom and peace of God, confessing my daily sins, believing in his forgiveness and grace, and noticing big differences in my attitudes and behaviors. I knew if God could change someone like me, he could change anyone, and I was eager to tell others about Jesus and his life-changing love.

As we settled into our new neighborhood, I went door-to-door inviting women to my home for an afternoon tea. I wanted to get to know my neighbors, and at the tea, I offered a six-week Bible class about Jesus from the book of Mark. The women were always interested. One dear, elderly lady who lived next door asked me to continue the lessons. Once a week, we would sit together on her little couch, and I never tired of telling her Bible stories and explaining the gospel to her. (When I use the word "gospel," I am referring to the good news message Jesus brought when he came to earth—the message that acceptance with God, forgiveness of sins, and eternal salvation can be ours through Jesus, because he paid the penalty for our sins when he died on the cross.)

Since I frequented the photocopy store making copies for the Bible lessons I taught, I became friends with the owner and offered to teach her the Mark lessons. She looked so happy when she understood that we are saved by grace and not by our own good effort. One day, I watched my short little friend bravely ask two Catholic nuns who came into the store if they knew about Ephesians 2:8–9: "For by grace you have been saved through faith. And this is not your own doing; it is the gift of God." She wanted to know why she had never been taught that truth in her religious school.

On the busy avenue near our mission office, a young lady sold candy. Whenever I walked by, I would stop at her small wooden kiosk and chat while buying my favorite chocolate cookies. After we were friends, I began to talk to her about Jesus. She loved the stories, but she resisted the gospel message. She felt she didn't deserve God's forgiveness because of something she had done in the past. I could see she was lonely and hungry for the peace and acceptance God gives, so I kept telling her about Jesus, at the same time taking her with me to church, to camp, and to my home.

When I heard there was a young American woman in the Cochabamba prison, I went to meet her. She was serving a sentence for the cocaine-related crimes of her drug-lord husband. For three years, I visited this beautiful blond and her two little boys, including them in the life of our family as much as I could, and sharing with her the stories of God's love and salvation.

On mini-buses, in parks, and in doctor's offices, I talked about God's grace. During youth camps, I had intentional conversations with teenage girls and invited them to my weekly Bible study. I made friends with the mothers of my children's friends and shared the gospel with them. At mission meetings, I challenged our colleagues to live by grace. I taught courses on grace at a small Bible seminary, and I spoke at retreats and

women's meetings, teaching that the good news of the gospel is for unbe-
lievers and believers alike. Telling others about Jesus and his love for sinners energized me!

While this new boldness truly amazed me, at the same time, I was
growing more aware of my pride. I was pushy, when I should have been
sensitive. I was domineering and thought everyone should listen to me,
when sometimes I should have been quiet. And I was critical and argu-
mentative with others who disagreed with me. I loved people, but not
like Jesus loves. These truths about myself became especially clear when
I read the biography of Dr. Kenneth Moynagh, *Man of Two Worlds.*

I saw this little book sitting on a shelf at our old mission-house
library—that wonderful, musty gathering of abandoned and out-of-print
books. I was intrigued because the author was Patricia St. John, a remarkable writer of creative children's fiction. It was because of her name that I
picked up the book. By page two, I was totally gripped. I wanted to know
more about this man; I wanted to be like him. I have read this book once
a year ever since.

Kenneth Moynagh was born into a family of Irish settlers in Kenya
around the beginning of the twentieth century. In those days, East Africa
was not an easy place to live. His mother went there from Ireland as a
single Protestant missionary. His father, an accountant and political figure, settled there after running away from Ireland to escape having to
enter a Catholic seminary. Ken, their second son, was a shy and athletic
child. When he was nine, the family moved to England. It was there, in a
boy's school, that he committed his life to Christ.

Ken became a certified doctor in 1938, then joined the Royal Army
Medical Corps with the idea of being a missionary when the war was
over. At an Officers' Christian Union meeting, he met his wife-to-be,
Wendy, and they were married in February of 1941. Ken was posted to

West Africa and separated from his wife and daughter for three-and-a-half unhappy years. Homesick and gripped with spiritual hunger, Ken was afraid to share his faith, yet he longed to be different.

Meeting some missionaries while in Africa, Ken looked to them for spiritual encouragement, but when he saw their strained relationships and colonial attitudes, he despaired. Then someone gave him a little magazine called *Rwanda Notes.* On the cover was a photograph of a white man and an African, talking and laughing together like brothers, illustrating an article about revival in East Africa. That picture—of the two men working together as equals and with obvious joy—was different from any missionary work he'd seen, and he yearned to be part of a community like that.

When Ken completed his military service, he and Wendy offered themselves to work with the Rwanda Mission, and in 1947 they moved to Africa. It was a typical mission station, with a church, a school, and a hospital. Ken, the only doctor, worked in the hospital with two English nurses and an African staff. He began with enthusiasm. He had so much to give. His African coworkers were respectful and glad to learn from him, yet Ken felt uneasy around them. They had something he lacked, and he resented it. He realized, "These men knew Jesus. They were not afraid to be themselves, because they themselves did not matter very much anymore."[1]

During his student days and the war years, Ken had lost the peace he had had when he first simply trusted Jesus. Now, he realized, he was striving to be an outstanding Christian. The effort it took to build and maintain his reputation—that of a self-controlled, successful missionary doctor—made him restless and edgy.

Ken sensed something was missing, so he asked the African Christians about their conversions. They told him of a visitor who had come to their homes eleven years earlier, not preaching, just talking with them about Jesus, and brokenness, and repentance. They confessed their sins that day—and never stopped. It was simple, they explained. They enjoyed a closeness with Jesus by continually admitting their sins and receiving his peace and joy.

At about the same time, Ken and Wendy were visited by some missionaries from Uganda who also displayed a vibrant, living relationship with the Lord Jesus. They, too, made a habit of quickly confessing any sin in their lives and receiving cleansing. Wendy realized they knew a secret she knew nothing about. She had been feeling defeated, hiding her failures behind a mask of pride and pretense, but God was working in her heart.

"I began to understand," Wendy said, "that when He convicts me of irritability, self-pity, and anger, all I have to say is, 'Yes, Lord, forgive me and cleanse me.' No more excuses or concealing, but an acceptance of self, a new day-by-day knowledge of Jesus and a tremendous sense of peace."[2] Wendy shared her fresh discovery with Ken, and he saw a new gladness about her, but he was not pleased. He was burdened with the hospital workload, and now he felt left behind by his wife.

One day Ken read Romans 9:33: "See, I lay in Zion a stone that causes men to stumble, and a rock that makes them fall." Ken wrote that he felt God say something like, "All your life you have been standing erect on this stone, hiding Jesus. Even when you've prayed for blessing, you really wanted success. Let go of your pride, fall on this stone, and be broken, and then people will begin to see Jesus. Otherwise, you will just go on as an ordinary orthodox missionary, grinding out the same message. Others will see you, not Jesus."[3]

Ken began to understand what it meant to be broken before God—acknowledging his pride, confessing his sins, and remembering Jesus' love and mercy shown by his death on the cross. His relationships at home and at the hospital began to change; instead of his normal, domineering personality, there was a new gentleness about him.

I used to pretend I was a missionary, until I decided to come down off the stage and be myself, a forgiven sinner. It was much more comfortable and the Africans liked it much better. One day I shared with them my deeper temptations of impurity, and they all began singing. I thought they must have misunderstood me, but no, they had understood perfectly and were praising God! "We never knew that the missionaries were just like us," they said.[4]

One story about the apostle Peter is repeated in all four of the Gospels. The night Jesus was arrested and taken away by soldiers, Peter was the only disciple who followed the crowd. All the other followers had fled for their lives. Although he tried to remain discreet, three distinct times he was recognized as a friend of Jesus. Three times he refuted the truth; he blatantly lied.

Just a few hours earlier, while reclined at their last meal together, Jesus had warned Peter, "Truly, I tell you this very night, before the rooster crows, you will deny me three times" (Matthew 26:34). Peter argued: "Even if I must die with you, I will not deny you!" (Matthew 26:35). So when the rooster crowed after Peter's third denial, he remembered Jesus' prediction, broke down, and "wept bitterly" (Matthew 26:75).

On that same night, another true drama played out. For thirty pieces of silver, Judas betrayed Jesus and led his enemies to him. Judas was filled with remorse as he saw Jesus being tortured and condemned to death. To appease his wrenching conscience, he returned the blood money to the Jewish leaders, confessing, "I have sinned by betraying innocent blood" (Matthew 27:4). The priests rebuffed him, with a that's-not-our-problem response. Judas, distraught, threw down the coins, ran out, and hanged himself.

Peter went out and wept bitterly.

Judas went out and committed suicide.

Sometime later, the resurrected Jesus himself came near to Peter in a marvelous way. Peter and his buddies had been fishing all night and had caught nothing. At dawn, as they neared the shore, they heard a man call out to them, "Children, do you have any fish?" (John 21:5). They told him no, and he told them to throw their nets on the right side of the boat and they would catch some. When they did as he said, their nets miraculously filled with fish. The disciple John then recognized Jesus and cried, "It is the Lord!" Peter jumped into the water and swam to Jesus, leaving the others to wrestle with the bulging nets of fish.

In the last chapter of the Gospel of John, we read the words spoken between Peter and Jesus there on the lakeshore. It seems Jesus had already forgiven Peter for his triple denial, for he never mentioned it. Instead, he asked him *three times*, "Peter, do you love me?" Peter answered *three times*, "Yes, I love you, Lord." Peter's relationship to Jesus was totally reestablished. That breakfast with Jesus was an unforgettable moment in Peter's life.

But what about Judas? Couldn't he have been restored? I like to think had he taken his guilt to Jesus rather than to the religious leaders, he would have found forgiveness. Remember when Judas led the soldiers to Jesus that dark night in the Garden of Gethsemane? Right after the kiss of betrayal, Jesus called him "friend" (Matthew 26:50). There it was, God's gift of repentance, held out to Judas in that word—yet he ignored it. He did not understand Jesus' mercy and grace, and his subsequent shame and hopelessness led him to end his own life.

All of us have both Peter *and* Judas in us. We're capable of committing great sins. The shame of our sin can depress us, as it did Judas. Our challenge is to believe, like Peter, in the grace and good news of the gospel and to hurry to Jesus whenever we sin. We *will* fail, but we mustn't fail to go to Jesus for forgiveness and peace. We mustn't miss the miracles, and the community, and the special words of love that he has for us, like he had for Peter.

Ken Moynagh's humble openness about his faults and failures became one of the secrets of his strength. Years later, when a young pastor came and poured out his heart to him in confession, he was shocked to hear Ken's reply:

> I am just the same. I've been defeated in the same way. I thought I should have to live with a bad conscience all my life but the turning point came when I was able to say to people, "This is the sort of man I was, and still am, apart from the saving, keeping grace of God." Rejoice and praise for victory but never forget! If you lose touch with your Saviour for one day, you may well find yourself back where you started. Because these are the sort of chaps that we were, are, and always could be—but we have a wonderful Saviour!"[5]

Ken met for prayer, confession, and praise early each morning with the African believers who worked on his mission compound. God did many wonderful things for the joyful crowds "in the little prayer hut that had become the center of Christian community ever since the first days of revival."[6] In one of his letters, Ken wrote:

> The missionaries were not onlookers. . . . Jesus drew near and convicted us. We do not regard ourselves . . . sent out to save pagan Africans. We are fellow-sinners and fellow-prisoners with them, and the same Jesus is setting us free. At times we have been guilty of ambition, the desire for a reputation, stubbornness, pride and jealousy. We have known the barrenness of busy lives and the busyness of barren lives, but He restores my soul . . . He is with me.[7]

Dr. Moynagh was a skilled gastric surgeon, his hospital work was strenuous, and the demand for his pastoral leadership in the Rwandan churches never ended, yet he became known for his unruffled, caring spirit. The years of the Moynaghs' last term of service in Africa were fruitful but difficult, with the many sorrows and anxieties that came because of a bloody civil war. So in 1964, they resigned from the mission and settled in England.

At St. Bartholomew's Hospital in London, Ken quickly gained a good reputation for diagnosing correctly and for his gracious attitude. Young people flocked to him for counseling, and he received many invitations to speak. His biographer wrote:

> His way of speech was diffident and his voice not easily heard, but his face was radiant and his manner authoritative. He never stood apart on a pedestal, but shared his weaknesses and failures freely. "I shall go back to work on Monday," he once told a large conference group, "and feel such a hypocrite, having said such high things here in this pulpit, but God sees me in Jesus, accepted in the Beloved."[8]

Ken approached every meeting with his characteristic confidence that the Lord had a message for each person. "Many are looking for new techniques and methods, instead of repentance. . . . The unsaved sinner has only one thing to do with sin and that is repent. And the experienced sanctified Christian has only one thing to do and that is repent. Repentance leads to forgiveness; forgiveness leads us to walking with God."[9]

During the summer of our return to Bolivia, I heard a pastor from Belfast, Ireland, speak on the topic of revival. He shared stories of past revivals in Britain and explained that true revival always starts with deep, corporate repentance. The desire of my heart became that there would be a dynamic spiritual awakening in Bolivia, among the mission community and the national church, and throughout the whole country.

I began to pray, asking God to do for us in Bolivia what he had done in Rwanda and Uganda. I longed for him to do a work in the hearts of others like he was doing in mine.

For answers to my prayers, I would have to wait, and I am still waiting. As of today, revival has not come to Bolivia. But I did my best to tell other believers about the importance of seeing our sins and taking them to Christ for forgiveness. I frequently felt like the odd man out. One missionary argued with me that since those of us who have been born again are "saints," we should not see ourselves as sinners anymore and we don't need to repent. Others felt like I focused on sin too much—it's depressing, it's morose, it's unhealthy, they told me. I didn't find many friends who wanted to live this way, continually confronting their sin and confessing. But God encouraged me through Ken Moynagh.

Life in Bolivia went on for the next twelve years; Johannah, Miah, Gaby, and Caris thrived in their classes at the mission school; Jake set his hands to his youth work; and I was deeply content keeping house, helping at camps, leading home Bible studies, and teaching Galatians at a seminary. I never tired of giving the gospel to others. I am grateful that God did use me during those years to lead others to Jesus, but I still had more growing down to do.

5
~

A Suffering

*It is the unfortunate creature who denies the existence of sin
in general and his own in particular who must go on carrying
it. The way to freedom consists in honest confession and
repentance opens our hearts to the Comforter.*
—JOY DAVIDMAN, *Smoke on the Mountain*

I love retreats. When I get away on a retreat, God usually has something special for me, so I was glad to attend our annual missionary women's weekend. I anticipated a fun time, but on the second day a simple question broadsided me. I was unaware God needed to probe deep into my soul to free and to comfort me.

I remember feeling like a contented cat, curled up in an overstuffed armchair in the great room of our mission guesthouse, enjoying being with old friends, singing new songs, and listening to the charming accent and wit of the speaker from England. She was a stout lady, a compelling teacher with impressive illustrations from her missionary life in mountainous Nepal. I don't remember her name, nor the theme of the retreat, but two things stuck in my mind. One is a funny story that has nothing to do with this chapter, but I want to tell it. The speaker said that when she finished her work and left Nepal, she told her househelper to choose something from her home as a good-bye gift. The Nepali lady chose her false teeth. Oh, no, no no, that would not do, the missionary told her. She must choose something else, because those teeth wouldn't possibly fit her. "But m'am, they do!" the househelper assured her. "I have tried them out!" (It really happened!)

The second thing I'll never forget about that retreat is something quite serious. The white-haired Britisher talked about four "c-words," attitudes most women know well: comparing, coveting, criticizing, and complaining. These self-centered attitudes are kissing cousins, she explained; they intertwine and support each other. When we compare ourselves with others, we become envious or critical, and we grumble about what God has not given to us, or has not done for us. *Well, that's nothing new. If she needs personal examples, I could tell a few stories.* My mind was beginning to drift, but then she started talking about Jesus and the cross and I sat up, curious. *I must have missed something. What does Jesus' suffering have to do with women's sinful attitudes?* I would soon see how the four "c-words" are signs of rebellion against God.

The speaker described in vivid detail the scene in the garden on the night Jesus was betrayed. Jesus knew he was going to die on the cross. He knew it would be horrible—the physical pain of crucifixion, and the emotional anguish of taking on his body the shame of all the evil in man. He knew the angry religious leaders were going to stir up the soldiers and the crowds of people to scorn him, beat him, mock him. He knew his friends, his followers, would run away and abandon him.

But the hardest part of his dying would be this: the wrath of his father God was going to be poured out on him and, for a time, he would feel the abandonment, the separation from God. Jesus had many reasons to be "greatly distressed and troubled" (Mark 14:33), and he said, "Father, if you are willing, remove this cup from me." Yet he immediately added, "Nevertheless, not my will, but yours, be done" (Luke 22:42).

The retreat speaker finished her talk by asking: "Is there any 'cup' in your life, any suffering that you have not accepted from God's hand?"

That question followed me home. As I lay in my bed later that night, I thought about Hannah.

I pictured the pale funeral tent with its single row of metal chairs. My parents, two friends, and Jake and I sat there, facing our pastor and a table where a small white casket rested. Into a grave given to us in our friends' family cemetery, we were about to place our daughter, our first-born. Her time to be born had warped into her time to die.

It was my first taste of real suffering.

Jake and I had been married for four years; I was twenty-seven years old, and we were ready and excited to be starting our family there in North Carolina. I dreamed of having lots of little kiddos, and I had relished carrying my growing baby inside me everywhere I went. Jake had enclosed the side porch on our cabin to make a tiny room, and I filled it up with a crib, a wooden rocking chair, and a small dresser—each drawer packed with perfectly folded tiny shirts, sleepers, and blankets in pastels of blue, green, and yellow. I was happily waiting for our baby.

While sitting in the last of our childbirth classes a week before our baby's due-to-arrive date, I was, of course, large in girth and grateful the end was near. But that night I was unable to concentrate on the labor and delivery film because my normally active in-utero baby was strangely still.

Earlier that week, I had been awakened by an uncomfortable shifting in my belly. The baby—I found out at the doctor's office the next morning—had twisted into a breech position. Her head, which for weeks had been down and ready to push her way out, was now up in my ribcage. The baby was fine, the doctor assured me. But he added a warning: If she did not flip back down, he may have to perform a Caesarean delivery.

Now, two days later, I sat in that class, uncomfortable, with the baby's head pressing against my ribs and noticing the lack of movement. Surrounded by those happy, nervous soon-to-be parents, I felt isolated. Worry weighed me down, and even though Jake was by my side, I didn't dare voice my fearful thought. *Is there something wrong with our baby?*

The next morning I pushed and stretched to get the baby to respond, but the eerie quietness in my womb continued. I called the doctor's office and his nurse consoled me, saying, "Babies sleep a lot near the end and don't move as much." I tried to rest in that hope, but by midday I was distraught. When Jake came home for lunch, we drove to see the doctor.

"This machine is very reliable." I'll never forget those words, whispered by my doctor as he sat down on his stool with the fetal Doppler stethoscope in hand. He had been trying for twenty minutes to find a heartbeat, searching all over my swollen abdomen. We heard none of the chugging-train sound we'd come to love. Only scratchy, empty static.

Five days later, labor began. After twelve hours, I delivered our tiny little girl. The doctor advised us to not look at her; he was protecting Jake and me, as he didn't know what she would look like after being dead for a week, or what it might take to deliver her feet-first. With my eyes clamped shut, I heard my doctor compassionately say, "It's a girl." My heart broke, and I curled up in a ball and wept, shaking and shameless. Oh, the sorrow! I would never see my little daughter. I would never hold my baby.

We named her Hannah Mary, and two days later we buried her.

When my parents gave me Joni Eareckson Tada's devotional book *Diamonds in the Dust,* I was pleased. I had read her autobiography, *Joni,* so I knew I could learn a lot from her experiences and thoughts. I kept the stocky little blue book on the corner hutch for several years and tried to read bits of her wisdom each morning to our family at the breakfast table.

Everyone should listen closely to what Joni Eareckson Tada says. Joni (pronounced "Johnny") has lived an incredible life: writing books, recording music, acting in a film about her life, producing art, hosting radio and television shows, serving on government committees, interviewing on national television, founding the *Joni and Friends* ministry to persons with disabilities, traveling around the world, teaching, preaching, and reaching out—all while seated in a wheelchair! Joni knows God, and he speaks loud through her. We would all do well to listen.

In 1967, having just graduated from high school, Joni dove into the Chesapeake Bay and broke her neck. Instantly, she went from being an active, athletic teenager to a quadriplegic, completely paralyzed from her shoulders down. For several years while in hospitals and rehab centers, Joni struggled through a deep darkness of anger, depression, bitterness, and confusion. She fought hard against God, against the idea that this could be his divine purpose for her life. But God won every battle. There came a day when she submitted to his plan, finally accepting that "God will permit what He hates to promote what He loves."[1]

As Joni slowly surrendered to him, God equipped her for her unique and necessary ministry work. For over forty years, through her movie and books and art and speaking events, she has encouraged thousands of people around the world, especially families affected with chronic illness and disability. God has used Joni as his spokeswoman in churches, at camps, conferences, and in government. She is an intelligent, winsome, joyful woman, constantly singing God's praises, and she works with a supernatural energy, inspiring and cheering and teaching others wherever she goes.

Here is some of her wisdom:

On Longings

God has good reasons for giving us such large appetites. He has placed within us desires and dreams in order to test us and to humble us, to see what is in our heart, to see whether or not we would follow Him. He causes us to hunger so that we might learn to feed on the Bread of Heaven, to live on every word that comes from the mouth of the Lord. Taste and see that the Lord is good; it is He who will fill you to satisfaction.[2]

On Contentment

Contentment is not found in circumstances. Contentment is found in a Person, the Lord Jesus. It requires a special act of grace to accommodate ourselves to every condition of life, to carry an equal temper of mind through every circumstance. Only in Christ can we face poverty contentedly, without losing our comfort in God. And only in Christ can we face plenty and not be filled with pride.[3]

On Purpose

Do you believe God has a wonderful plan for your life? If not, let Psalm 57 jar your memory. Find assurance in the first few verses. God will fulfill His purpose for you. He'll do it *for* you because He keeps His promise. He'll fulfill His plan *in* you by creating in you the image of His Son. Also He will fulfill His plan *through* you as you touch others with His love.[4]

After the shock of Hannah's death, I didn't know what I would do with my days. My dream to be a happy stay-at-home mom with a nursing baby was traumatically crushed. But God revealed a gracious plan. Several of my friends asked me to keep their preschoolers for a few hours in the mornings. I borrowed children's books and music from the library, our church let me use the nursery room, and *voila!*—I was the director and only staff worker of a half-day childcare center, responsible for five to seven little girls. I called it the Montreat Morning School. It later became a real preschool, and it's still running today, almost thirty-five years later! The hugs and smiles from those precious children softened my sadness. Then God gave me my heart's desire: our daughter Johannah Helen was born eleven months after we buried Hannah.

I thought I'd made peace with Hannah's death. But during consequent years, whenever I told her story, I relived the pain and cried. I liked my tears;

they were the mark of my great love and my tender soul—or so I thought. They also brought me the attention and sympathy I craved. But as I lay in bed that night after the women's retreat in Bolivia, with that question heavy on my heart and mind—*Is there any cup in your own life, any suffering that you have not accepted from God's hand?*—I saw for the first time that my tears were often self-centered, and there was bold unbelief in my heart.

Just as Jesus' death was God's perfect will, so my baby's death must be part of his good and perfect will for me.

I had been attributing Hannah's death to Satan, knowing God would never kill a baby. So in my mind it followed that Satan had won—his will had been done, so he must be more powerful than God. How could I trust a God like that? I was angry at the injustice of Hannah's death. *Why did God allow my baby to die when there were so many abortions?* I felt betrayed. *Why did God let me carry her full-term, then die an unexplainable death?* The cause of her death had been listed as *anoxia*, a lack of oxygen, yet the autopsy showed she was perfectly formed. The umbilical cord was healthy, with no knots and no wrapping around her neck.

Unconsciously, I had believed the lie that God is not always good.

According to the retreat speaker, it wasn't too late to take the cup of suffering God had given me fourteen years earlier. I needed to accept Hannah's death as from God's good hand. I confessed my sins of anger and bitterness, of not trusting him, and of thinking that he is not good. With silent tears, I admitted I had not accepted Hannah's death as his will for my life. Lying there in my bed that dark night, with only God seeing, I lifted my empty palm and took the cup.

Although Joni Eareckson is a quadriplegic and well-acquainted with suffering, she doesn't excuse her sin or exempt herself from the need for ongoing repentance. Frequently in her devotional entries, Joni writes about sin in general—and about her own sin in particular:

As an old Puritan once advised, "Sit close to self-scrutiny." It's the best way to fully appreciate what Jesus accomplished for us on the cross. Only an honest view of our sin will give us a full appreciation of God's mercy. Remember Christ did not simply die for the general sins of the world; He died specifically for your specific sin.[5]

Sometimes I get so weary of my sin that I cry, "What a wretched person I am!" I look forward to the day when I'll no longer transgress against my loving Lord, when I'll be free from this body of sin and death. *Lord, please possess me so that all my thoughts and desires rise to You. . . . May I hate my sin as You hate it . . . may I grow to love Your law as You love it. Brighten my hope that soon there will be no more sin, and I will at last find final completeness in You!*[6]

Some of my friends tell me I'm too hard on myself. They say I berate myself. But I know the truth. I know when I am vying for attention or shading the truth. I know when I am deliberately ignoring the Spirit's direction. I know the times when I turn my back in anger to hurt someone. As the psalmist says in Psalms 51:3, I *know* my transgressions. Sensitivity to sin is not a curse but a blessing.[7]

Six months after Hannah's burial, a cold blast of grief hit me. I felt as if no one on earth missed her except me, and there was nothing tangible to show that she had even lived. I needed something—something to hold in my hands to share with others—so I created a scrapbook, pasting in the cards and letters of sympathy we'd received. As I penned her name and its meaning on the title page—*Hannah* means "grace" and *Mary* means "bitter"—I had an epiphany. I felt comforted by hope, born of the knowing that her life and death had purpose and God was fulfilling the meaning of her name, the purpose of her life.

Hannah had brought a message from God, a message of grace, albeit a bitter one. God gave me a small taste of bitter sorrow in exchange for some great lessons of grace. He gave me a real sense of the nearness of heaven and the brevity of earthly life. He helped me grieve, while proving his love for me through little girls and through the gift of another baby. He gave me the privilege of starting a nursery school that blessed, and still blesses, many children and families. He equipped me to help others in their grief, making me unafraid to move close to the brokenhearted and be a quiet presence in their pain.

Once I accepted my cup of suffering from God, fourteen years after Hannah's burial, I never again shed pain-filled, self-pitiful tears over her. When I tell her story, if tears come, they are clean from bitterness and mixed with gratitude to God for what Hannah's life and death has taught me. And when I think about her, I long for the day when I will see her again. I imagine her running up to me in heaven, taking my hand and leading me to Jesus. That'll be the day!

Most importantly, through Hannah, God taught me to believe the truth Joni Eareckson Tada espouses: God permits things he *hates*, to accomplish things he *loves*.

Not only do I admire Joni for her beautiful model of grace in suffering, but I also am attracted to her honest and open confession of sin and her genuine, contagious joy in Jesus. In *Diamonds in the Dust*, she writes,

> There are countless times when I get impatient . . . small irritations. . . . I get mad at others, also mad at myself for failing to hold my tongue. Soon the spat is forgotten and God has hardly entered into it. We have a way of sweeping small sins under the carpet of our conscience without ever considering how they affect God. . . . Perhaps our problem is that we do not take sin seriously enough.

She closes that day's devotional with a prayer expressing her desire to bring all sin, small sins especially, before God in sincere confession. *"Help me to take sin . . . seriously."*[8]

God continues to teach me through Joni. My experience with suffering, grief, and loss seems paltry compared to Joni's daily challenges. How dare I put my story next to hers? I dare, in order to say this: sometimes my suffering is prolonged by my own fault. Sometimes I indulge my anger and self-pity; I complain, I blame, I fume. My sin blocks God's power to perform healing in my heart. I see through Joni's example that suffering does not exempt me from the need to name and turn from my sins. On the contrary, sometimes God *uses* suffering to reveal where I fall short, to facilitate deeper repentance, to give a higher joy, and to heal and prepare me for greater service, just as he has done for Joni.

I continued to wonder, *Do I take my sins seriously? All of them?* Fortunately, God continued to make sure that I would.

6
~

A New Seeing

Quite frankly, I'm sick to death of ideals and I've been so
frustrated by them I really don't care anymore. What I am
looking for is a savior—not someone who will tell me what I
ought to be, but someone who will forgive me for what I am,
and then with his very love enable me to be more than I ever
believed I could be. It's exactly that that Jesus does.

—BRUCE THIELEMANN, *Telltale Tears*

"Are you immobilized?" My friend's question nailed me. She had been watching as I called out to my four-year-old to stop playing in our forested backyard and come in for her afternoon nap. My little daughter Caris was completely ignoring me and I stood there, staring at her out the sliding glass door—yes, I was indeed immobilized. I did not know what to do.

Following my metamorphis that day on I-40, God's gracious love had been transforming my thoughts, and I had begun to doubt my mothering ability. I knew I needed to discipline my children and uphold standards of behavior, but how could I do that with grace? I wanted my girls to know God's love and acceptance as I was coming to experience it. I longed to guide them with tender mercy and kindness. I wanted to reach their hearts, not just respond to their outward actions, but I didn't know how. I didn't even know how to get my little daughter to come inside the house without losing my cool.

God is not like your mother. That phrase came into my head on one of those days of struggling, and that truth delights and comforts me still. It is not referring to my own mother; it is about me. When I repeated the phrase "God is not like your mother" to my girls, it was to make sure they learned that God is not like *me*.

I guess it was obvious. I'm human, and I get tired, cranky, sour, and selfish. When my daughters were young, I wasn't always a good listener; I was often distracted with all the work piled around in the kitchen and on the floor by the washing machine. At times I was oversensitive, over-reactive, and demanding, wanting more help and appreciation from my girls. I craved their love and attention and expected them to understand me and fulfill my needs. When they disobeyed me or hurt one another, I was often shocked. *You did what?!* Sometimes it was hard to forgive them. Sometimes I was harsh. I wanted to be a good mom—a great mom—but I failed, over and again.

Oh, how I wanted my girls to know how different God is: never demanding, never too busy, without a single selfish need, unshocked by sin. Always gentle and kind. Always patient and forgiving. All-wise and all-knowing. God forgives, he forgets, and unlike me, he's generous with acceptance and grace. That's why it gave me great joy to remind them—and myself: God is not like your mother.

I loved being a stay-at-home mom with my four little women, Johan-nah, Miah, Gabrielle, and Caris. When they were small, of course, there were days I desperately needed help from friends with strong nerves who could care for them so I could get away. But most of the time, I treasured the freedom and privilege of mothering without having to work outside the home—reliving my own childhood (playing and swimming, taking hikes, making crafts), re-seeing life through their young eyes (watching clouds, reading books out loud, enjoying art and rain and milkshakes every Sunday), and re-appreciating the beauty of sharing life together (beds and laughter, tears and chocolate cake, songs, and being at camp). It was fun being their mom!

But after my grace awakening in 1991, I faced a different sort of challenge. Up until then, I had been following the childrearing advice from the popular Christian experts of the day; I was focused on my children's behaviors. I wanted the Wetzel girls to be *shiny good*, so others would think well of our family and of me. My systems and ideas led to a self-focused, godless cycle. When the girls were good, I felt proud. When they were not, I felt responsible. Everything depended on me, myself, and I. My expertise or lack of it. My doing the right thing, so my girls would do the right thing.

After I was spiritually freed and I truly believed I could do nothing to earn God's grace—"For by grace you have been saved through faith. And this is not your own doing; it is the gift of God" (Ephesians 2:8-9)— I wanted my girls to receive this great gift and live free also. Rule-keeping and demanding outward obedience from them became odious and I feared their becoming little hypocrites like I had been. I wanted to reach their hearts with grace like God had reached mine. But how?

Funny, it wasn't a book on parenting that helped me; it was a little book by Roy Hession, *We Would See Jesus*. A book that gave me a new way of seeing.

Roy Hession had been a successful evangelist in England for many years when he felt a loss of God's power in his daily life. "A terrible experience!" he wrote. "I was like that son of the prophets in Elisha's school who lost his axe head while chopping down a tree, but who perhaps for a few strokes at least continued to chop with the handle and wondered why he was making no progress with his work."[1] Hession continued to preach, doubling his efforts, and trying to use force and intensity to persuade others to follow Jesus Christ—but with little result.

In 1947, Hession invited leaders of the East African Church to come to England for a conference he was organizing. He was curious about the revival they were experiencing in Rwanda and he wanted others to know about it. As the African pastors told stories and shared their message, their humility and joy contrasted sharply with his sense of heaviness. He watched as others, his wife included, humbled themselves and received cleansing, forgiveness, and a fresh filling of Jesus' Spirit. Hession could not see that his spiritual dryness was connected to his need for repentance.

The African pastors confronted him in love, suggesting he begin by repenting of his selfish attitudes toward his wife. They had noticed he treated her coldly, as if she were only his secretary. God opened his eyes, and Hession was broken by what he saw. When he repented, God filled him with joy and power. He said "It was like beginning my Christian life all over again."[2]

Hession had to unlearn what he had been teaching others about sin and grace. "I had been trying to get from God the power and blessing I needed by my own works, rather than coming to the cross of Jesus for the cleansing of His blood. I had been struggling instead of repenting."[3] As Hession walked in this new way of humility, God showed him more of his shortcomings, and more of Jesus. In *We Would See Jesus*, Hession describes how beautiful Jesus is. Seeing and knowing Jesus is the same as seeing and knowing God, and seeing and knowing God is the whole purpose of life.

Like Roy Hession, I had much to unlearn. As I read and reread *We Would See Jesus*, I realized I didn't know God as he truly is, nor had I understood the true purpose of my life. "God is unknowable unless He grants us a revelation of Himself,"[4] Hession wrote, and that is exactly what he did in Jesus—revealed himself. "Nowhere else can we fully see God but in the face of Jesus Christ."[5] To know God, we must see Jesus. Jesus as all we need. Jesus as the Truth. Jesus as the Door. Jesus as the Way. Jesus as the End.[6] Knowing Jesus and worshiping him is the whole purpose of our life.

Roy Hession guided me through a new world. I thought God was justifiably disgusted with me when I messed up. At the same time, I believed Jesus always had warm compassion for me no matter what I did. I had separated God and Jesus in my mind. The truth is that God the Father and Jesus the Son are one; they have all the same qualities. God is never angry with me, because he poured out his wrath on Jesus, and he completely forgives me for all my sins—past, present, and future. God always sees me with the compassionate eyes of Jesus.

According to Hession, God didn't send Jesus into the world to bring good advice but good news. What news is that? At Jesus' birth, the angel of the Lord announced these words: "Fear not, for behold, I bring you *good news* of great joy" (Luke 2:10, italics mine). As Hession wrote:

> So this is what we ought to be hearing in our churches—good news! But we hear precious little of it. What usually passes for good news is all too often good advice, with very little good news about it. The weakness of good advice is that we ourselves are weak, we just cannot follow it. In any case, it almost certainly comes too late: the things counseled against have already been done. It helps as much as shutting the stable door after the horse had bolted. But when Jesus comes to us, He does not come with good advice, but rather with good news. He does not say, "Do this, don't do that," but rather "You've done them already but I have good news for you." What news? "Be of good cheer, your sins are forgiven."[7]

That was exactly what I needed to hear over and over, the good news of God's love for sinners. This gospel truth reformed my parenting ideas.

Slowly, I learned to see God in the face of Jesus and began to know and accept that he is never frowning at me; he does not keep a record of my sins; he always has good news for anyone who fails—and repents. I would need to keep my heart and mind focused on Jesus and his love, at the same time giving the good news to my children so they could live in the freedom of the God's unconditional love, too. Of course, it was a process, and many times I failed to live it out.

On one particular afternoon, when I was busy on the computer finishing a project for camp, one of my daughters burst into the office insisting I take her to the orthodontist at once. She knew she was expected to walk the seven blocks to her appointment, but this was the child who was notorious for refusing to look at clocks. I had no mercy. "No. You can walk."

"But I'll be late!" she whined.

I said something along the line of, "Tough cookies, it's your own fault. Just go and leave me alone." She left in a huff, and I sat there, smug.

The house got quiet, but my noisy heart condemned me. I could clearly see my impatience and lack of mercy toward my daughter, but instead of repenting, I decided to go find her and make amends. Out on the sidewalk, I met her as she was coming back from the dentist. It was an awkward encounter. I spit out something like "I was wrong to get angry with you, but I am under a lot of pressure. I need you to understand, I have a lot to do . . ."

She responded with something like "Whatever, Mom." My explanation and excuses mended nothing.

We were deadlocked for two days. I felt justified, thinking, *I did my part.* But my daughter stayed icy and far removed from me. It took time before I was able to bow my heart and ask God to show me my sin. He brought to my mind the words "selfish ambition," which I found in James 3:16 and 17: "For where jealousy and selfish ambition exist, there will be disorder and every vile practice. But the wisdom from above is first pure, then peaceable, gentle, open to reason, full of mercy and good fruits."

My heart sank. My sins were not just impatience and blame; I had been demanding that my daughter bend and support me. I was jealous for my own agenda, and I totally lacked gentleness, reason, and mercy. My sins had piled up, blocking my peace with God, myself, and my child like the thick adobe walls in our home. With God's forgiveness, I could now make true amends with my daughter. This time I offered no excuses. I confessed to her my sadness that I had treated her harshly, admitted my selfish ambition, and asked her to forgive me. She did.

Oh, there were other times. With another of my teenage daughters, I became irritated and resentful because her life was too busy and full to include the rest of us. I felt she took advantage of the shelter and food of our home, like a car uses a gas station. She rarely had time to be with us, let alone to straighten up her room or help with cooking and dishes. Her friends got the best of her, and yes, I was jealous and bitter.

One afternoon, she buzzed in and was about to buzz out—and I blew up. I explained to her in a sharp tone how her actions were hurting the family. She took it with her characteristic calmness, gave me a self-righteous apology, went out the door, and that was that. I stayed angry.

Later that week, I realized something. Wasn't I like my daughter, doing what I wanted to do, running my own life? And hadn't I been *just* like her when I was her age—a self-absorbed teenager, blind to the effects of my selfishness on others? I went to her to ask for forgiveness for my resentment. She forgave me, but she didn't ask me to forgive her. So, I then had a choice to make; I chose to forgive her in my heart for being blind to her own faults. I was learning that I had to be willing to be the only sinner in the house, regardless of whether others were ready to repent along with me. I could only hope and pray that someday she would see Jesus as I was learning to see him and be willing to give him her sin.

It did happen—on God's timetable, not mine. About a year later, she had a beautiful change of sight and a deep repentance.

One of my favorite Bible stories is about David and Mephibosheth. David had been king for many years when he asked this question: "Is there still anyone left of the house of Saul, that I may show him kindness for Jonathan's sake?" (2 Samuel 9:1).

David was informed that there was indeed a relative still alive: Jonathan's son, named Mephibosheth. Jonathan had been David's dear friend; perhaps David had even met his little boy at one time. Second Samuel 4 tells about the night Mephibosheth's grandfather, Saul, and his father, Jonathan, were killed in battle. When Mephibosheth's nurse heard the news, she snatched him up and ran for their lives. Verse 4 says, "And as she fled in her haste, he fell and became lame."

Now Mephibosheth was a grown man, living in a place called Lo Debar. Lo Debar means "nothing." He was King Saul's grandson, born into privilege and wealth, but hiding in Lo Debar, living in "nothing."

David sent for Mephibosheth, and Mephibosheth responded. It couldn't have been easy in those days for a disabled person to travel. How did he move through the cobbled courtyards, maneuver the expansive halls, and enter the king's throne room? Did someone push him along in a wheeled chair? Did he use crutches? The Bible only tells us that as Mephibosheth came near to King David, he fell on his face. Then David said, "Mephibosheth! Do not fear, for I will show kindness for the sake of your father Jonathan and I will restore to you all the land of Saul your father and you shall eat at my table always" (2 Samuel 9:6–7).

What if Mephibosheth had kept hiding in Lo Debar? What if he had let fear keep him from making that journey? He would never have known about King David's gracious offer to restore his rightful inheritance. And what if he had been too proud or too ashamed to accept the king's offer? He would have missed life in the palace, friendship with the king, and daily dining at the royal table. His son, Mica, who moved to the palace with him (2 Samuel 9:13), would have missed all of that, too. But neither fear, nor pride, nor shame kept him away. Mephibosheth answered David's summons, and both he and his son were greatly blessed.

I love this story because I am like Mephibosheth. Motherhood offers me many occasions to feel lame with fear, pride, or shame. I could be undone by the guilt alone! But just like King David beckoned Mephibosheth to his throne, so Jesus invites me, just as I am, to his "throne of grace . . . and find help in time of need" (Hebrews 4:16). And he invites my children with me. I was a needy mom and, as Roy Hession wrote in *We Would See Jesus*, "Where there is need, there is God. Where there is sin, there is Jesus—seeking to forgive sin and cover all the damage that it has caused. He is not shocked at human failure; rather He is at home in it, drawn by it, knowing what to do about it, for He in Himself . . . is the answer to it all."[8]

What a marvelous truth. God loves sinners. The more I recognize my need for God, the more I seek his forgiveness, and the closer I become to him. God not only forgives me and changes me, he uses my life to display his grace and love. Also he promises to take all of my mothering mistakes and all the harm I have done and somehow in his sovereign wisdom and power turn them into good in my children's lives.[9] That makes me feel like jumping for joy!

I pray that my children will be like Mephibosheth's son, Mica, enjoying all the blessings of belonging to the King. I pray they, and *their* children, will stay near to Jesus, basking in his grace and living in freedom from fear, guilt, and shame. I pray they will imitate me in this one thing: practicing repentance and worshiping Jesus, focusing on him rather than on their mistakes. And I hope someday I will see big smiles on my daughters' faces, as they tell their own children, "God is not like your mother."

The season of full-time mothering ended gradually for me, like busy summer days that shorten and cool into fall. One by one, our daughters left for college.

When Caris was the only one still at home, God began to open my eyes to a complicated problem in my marriage. It was time to learn a different sort of repentance.

7
~

A Healing

*Couples don't fall out of love so much as
they fall out of repentance.*
GARY THOMAS, *Sacred Marriage*

"Have you and Jake always been so lovey-dovey?" my young American neighbor asked. I was flattered. And amazed. *Wow. She sees us as lovey-dovey?* If she only knew . . .

Ours has not been an easy marriage. We had a happy start; our first date was a bike ride in a cool October rain and we were married on a balmy spring day the following March. We were so in love—and also young, dumb, and unprepared for the lifetime commitment of marriage. When an impetuous, friendly, strong-minded Texas city girl like me marries a methodical, outdoorsy, gentle Michigan farm boy like Jake, there's bound to be friction. Big sparks, smoldering fires, and some serious-degree burns, too.

Only one month after our 1974 wedding, I remember looking at Jake as he slept next to me one morning and thinking, *Who is this stranger? What have I done?* It seemed clear I'd made the biggest mistake of my life, and since divorce is a shameful option for newlyweds, I felt stuck.

Fortunately for us, God has kept us stuck together; he has helped us at every difficult point. After our first emotional-roller-coaster year, he took us out of the challenging situation in Wisconsin and gave us a fresh start in North Carolina. We had some good years working together on a college campus, but by our seventh anniversary, after having two small daughters, our relationship was strained and I was feeling isolated from Jake. God miraculously provided a marriage retreat, which inspired the brilliant plan of quarterly Jake-and-Sarah getaways. Going out to dinner once a week wasn't working for us. I desired blocks of quality time with Jake; he enjoyed hiking and canoeing with me, so for many years, once each season—fall, winter, spring, and summer—we left our girls with friends and had a twenty-four-hour adventure. Now we have a unique collection of romantic memories made during those busy children-in-the-home years.

Our eighteenth year was a tough one, too, due to anger and discouragement in my soul. On the weekend of that anniversary, re-reading the framed calligraphy of our marriage vows, I felt ashamed at how often I'd failed to keep the promises I made at our wedding. Problems and weaknesses in our marriage continued through the years but I had no clue how to fix them. By the time we'd finished our thirtieth year, we had settled into some anemic, unhealthy patterns, but I'd convinced Jake and myself that compared to most couples we were good, we were doing *okay*.

But God intervened and showed us otherwise. I'm glad he did not leave us as we were.

Jake and I, and our youngest daughter, Caris, had gone to visit our two daughters who were then living in Spain. It was physically grueling for me, a rushed spring-break week that included three days in Morocco. One day, after a sweet and savory experience in the home of a friend in Casablanca—eating lamb couscous with our fingers, resting on pillows around the low table, sipping thick, minty Moroccan tea—we went to see the world-famous mosque. We didn't have much time before our bus departure, so we quickly circled the mosque, craning our necks to ooh and aah at the artistic mosaic patterns on pillars and arches and towers. Winding our way through the touristy crowds and the pervasive incense, we crossed the plaza to find a taxi for the bus station.

Then, *crash!* Right there in Moroccan public, we had a family meltdown. The subject of the disagreement was minor—something about deciding where to go next—compared with the anger that erupted. Jake and I sort of tried to talk it out, but I couldn't get him to see that the argument was his fault, not our daughter's. At the same time, he insisted my need to control was to blame. As we five crowded into a little taxi, I eyed my daughter's pinched face and felt sick to my stomach. *Not again*, I sighed. Despair and silence overtook me.

The next day, we ferried over to Spain and caught a train back to Granada, hardly speaking to each other. Even on the long flight home, my lips were sealed. My mind was jabbering, though, filled with agonizing thoughts and fear. *What is going to happen to us? How can we keep on living together, hurting each other like this?* When I let myself look back over the previous three or four years, I couldn't ignore the evidence that our relationship had been weakening. We had serious problems, and the big one that connected them all was this: we didn't know how to talk out a conflict. God knows how desperate I felt. *Where can we go for help? Can we even* **be** *helped?*

Oh, I wish I had the space to recount all the details of those next few weeks. All I can say here is this: God providentially connected us with Healing for the Nations.

Healing for the Nations (HFN) is a unique Christian counseling ministry started by Steve and Rujon Morrison. Steve is a musician and an Episcopal minister; Rujon is a discerning counselor and insightful teacher. As the daughter of a psychiatrist, Rujon grew up on the grounds of a mental institution where she was prepared for her life's calling in the mental and spiritual health field. Working as the educational director at a secular psychiatric hospital, during a staff discussion about the "useless faith" of a Christian patient, Rujon felt God say to her, "I want to heal My people. Put Me to the test."[1]

Years later, the Morrisons were invited to be a part of the church staff of St. Thomas' Church of England. After much prayer, they surrendered their corporate careers and moved to Lancaster, England to help with pastoral care and counseling. Their unique, retreat-based, Christ-centered therapy ministry began there.

Rujon and Steve believed the call to England was for a lifetime, but God had other plans. After two-and-a-half years, they were asked to establish a retreat ministry in Colorado. This turn in the road caught them by surprise, but they knew God was in it. In 1993, they moved to Colorado Springs and established their non-profit organization, which has been operating ever since. Now they are based in Kansas.

The heart of their ministry is an intensive retreat with worship times, classes, small group sessions, and creative activities. The main focus of their teaching is to help retreat participants open their hearts and allow God to expose the lies in their belief systems that distort how they see themselves, others, and God himself. The retreats are designed for each participant to experience the fullness of God's love, as shown by Jesus' sacrifice on the cross.

"We are all on a God journey to find out who he is and who we are in him," Rujon would say. "There is a war going on between our hearts and our heads. Even though our heads know the truths of God's love and acceptance, we unconsciously live out of fear and shame. But how can we live out of love when we don't know what love is?"[2]

Jake and I were on the journey, the God journey, about to experience his love and acceptance is new ways. This was in May, only a month after our Spain trip. Jake went first to the HFN weeklong retreat, and came home full of confidence and joy, a changed man—so completely altered that our seventeen-year-old daughter asked, "Who is this guy, and what did they do with my dad?" And she wasn't kidding.

Then it was my turn, and I was not disappointed. It was a glorious week, full of surprising insights and abundant hope. One of the first classes addressed the poisonous darts all of us carry in our spirit. Through the creative assignments, I was able to remember back to circumstances and events in my childhood and identify negative messages I had received— painful messages, such as *You don't belong. You're stupid. You will fail. You don't matter. You're all alone.* These phrases have been repeated in my psyche throughout my whole life, inflicting pain and shame, jerking me around, persuading me to manipulate my actions and try to control others in order to prove I do belong. I'm not stupid. I do matter.

Now I understood why, when Jake came into my life, his desire for me to be his wife made me feel loved, accepted, and important. I couldn't wait to marry him. But shortly after the wedding, as I continued to look to Jake to make me feel wonderful, of course, he couldn't. And vice versa. We couldn't possibly give each other all the approval we craved, so we had this unhealthy thing going on, kind of like living in a boxing ring, staying mostly in our corners to avoid being bruised. But through HFN, God showed us how to climb out of the ring.

I learned that each lie I'd listened to represented one of my God-given basic needs:

> Lie: *I don't belong.* = My need for belonging.
> Lie: *I am stupid and I will fail.* = My need for success.
> Lie: *I don't matter.* = My need for significance and worth.
> Lie: *I'm alone.* = My need for companionship.

God promises to meet all my needs. He wants to comfort me, heal me of the shame, and give me truths to refute the lies. That is what he did for Jake and me at our retreats. He truly changed us. But just as I faced a letdown following my wedding, I was devastated a few months after our retreats. Jake and I couldn't hang on to the truth. We were right back in the boxing ring.

We know the story of Adam's and Eve's failure to obey God. We know the consequences they suffered. But do we see any grace in their story? Here's my summary of Genesis 1, 2, and 3:

It all starts with God. Out of nothing, God creates the world: the skies, the land, the seas, and a beautiful garden sanctuary with an incredible variety of plants, trees, and creatures. He fashions two magnificent humans and gives them a satisfying purpose for their lives, balancing their calling—zoological work—with the pleasure of his daily company.

Then the evil Satan, disguised as a snake, entices Eve to question God's goodness. "Did God actually say, 'You should not eat of any tree in the garden?'" he asks her (Genesis 3:1). Eve answers him correctly; she quotes God: "We may eat of the fruit of the trees in the garden, but God said, "You shall not eat of the fruit of the tree that is in the midst of the garden . . . lest you die" (v. 2).

Next, Satan implies to Eve that God lied to her, telling her she won't die, that God is withholding something from her and therefore God is not good, and that actually if she were to eat the fruit, she would be as wise as God. This is a conversation Eve could ignore, but she doesn't. Satan's words, like poisonous darts, make her doubt God, and she is curious. So she goes to take another look at the forbidden tree. The fruit looks delightful, and who wouldn't want to be wise like God? So she plucks one piece of fruit—no, she plucks *two* pieces of fruit. One she eats, and one she gives to Adam.

Wow. Their eyes open, just as Satan promised. But it's not with wisdom; it's with the reality of their weakness, their vulnerability, their nakedness. Both Eve and Adam suddenly feel ashamed.

In the cool of that afternoon, as is his custom, the Lord comes walking in the garden looking for Adam and Eve. When he finds them hiding from him, he questions them. To Adam: "Where are you?" (v. 8), "Who told you that you were naked? Have you eaten of the tree of which I commanded you not to eat?" (v. 11). And to Eve: "What is this that you have done?" (v. 13). In answering, Adam tries to blame both God and Eve: "The woman whom you gave to be with me, she gave me fruit" (v. 12). And Eve claims it is Satan's fault: "The serpent deceived me" (v. 13).

I wonder why God did not ask them why they hid or why they disobeyed. I wonder why it's always easier for us to see someone else's sin rather than our own. I always wonder about such things, but let's turn back to Genesis.

After hearing their responses, God first curses the serpent, then pronounces judgment on their sin: To Eve, pain in childbirth and trouble in marriage. (That's how I view his words, "Your desire shall be for your husband and he shall rule over you" in verse 16.) And then to Adam: the ground cursed with thorns, thistles, and hard work (vv. 17–19). They must accept the dreadful consequences of their sin—the worst, being driven out of the garden and losing their daily visit with God.

Where is God's grace in this story? Preachers tell us it's in the promise of Christ hidden in the curse of the serpent, "He shall bruise your head" (v. 15), and that is true. Jesus took the punishment for our sin when he died on the cross, and we can escape the ultimate consequence of our sin—forever separation from God—if we put our trust in Christ. But I see more grace in this story, a daily grace. Even though the omniscient God knew Adam and Eve had sinned, he went looking for them. With his seeking, with his questions, God was giving them the chance to confess and repent of their sin. It wouldn't have changed all the consequences, but perhaps if they had been able to admit their wrongdoing they could have continued their afternoon walks with the Lord.

But the point I want to make is not about Adam and Eve; it is about God. God knows everything about us. He sees our rebellion, and he comes looking for us, wherever we may be hiding. He seeks the guilty, the failed, the undeserving. Why does he do that? I don't have to wonder why on this one, because I know . . . God is love.

At HFN, I learned a method of paying attention to my spirit, a simple tool I call "discipling my own heart." It took a few years of digging with this tool for me to be able to live in the fullness of God's love like I had experienced at my retreat. This tool guides me to a different sort of repentance—a repentance that leads to dependence on God to heal inner wounds caused by lies. It works like this:

When I have a conflict with or a negative reaction toward Jake (or anyone), I sit down. Sitting down is harder than you think, but it is the key to this process. I must sit down and by prayer invite God into my situation, using these questions:

- What just happened?
- What am I feeling?
- What am I thinking?
- What am I doing?

Notice, I don't ask myself any "why" questions; this is not about understanding or defending myself. It's about getting to the root of feelings, thoughts, and reactions. I write out the answers to these questions, then ask Jesus to show me which trap I am in—approval, performance, blame, or shame—and what lies are keeping me in those traps.

When I pinpoint a specific lie in my thinking, I do NOT do these things: Repeat a Scripture I know. Count my blessings. Think positively. Talk myself out of believing the lie. Blame Satan. Those options are self-propelled and essentially leave God out of the process, so I don't do any of that . . . *yet*.

Instead, first, I repent. I write a prayer of confession to God, asking him to forgive me for believing a lie. Second, I wait. I wait for God to give me a specific word for that specific lie.

God always has a healing word for me. It might be a Scripture verse or a song; a random truth that comes into my mind; or the very word I need to hear comes on the radio, in a conversation with a friend; or from the sighting of something in the garden. As long as what I "hear" lines up with the truths in the Bible, I take it as from God, spoken just for me. With his personal word comes the comfort of knowing God is near. I feel affirmed and loved, and God's love heals.

May I give an example? Shortly after we'd returned to Bolivia after our home assignment, after our HFN retreats and our amazing trans- formations had disappeared, Jake was gone to camp for a few days and I was home alone. His early morning phone call got me out of bed. *Sweet,* I thought. *It's my dear husband thinking of me.* The phone connection was splotchy, and Jake was short and to the point: "Sarah, when you come this weekend, please bring me two pairs of clean underwear. Bye."

As I put the phone down, I started fuming. *All he wants is under- wear. Is that all I am good for?* It sounds humorous to me typing this out, but it was not funny at the time! Before going out for my morning walk, I sat down with my Bible and journal and asked God to show me what was going on inside. It came down to feeling lonely and unloved. *I am alone,* and *No one cares* were the lies I identified. In my journal, I confessed them to God.

Then I went out to walk. A few blocks up from our house, standing at the intersection before crossing the busy street, I glanced at a billboard. It was an ad for Pepsi with a picture of two lovers and the simple words *Juntos, La Verdad.* meaning "Together, That's the Truth." I was looking for truth and there it was. In the span of time it takes for a green light to turn red, God said, loudly and largely, *You are not alone. I am right here. We are together. That is the truth.* He put this huge billboard in my path to make sure I wouldn't miss his word. It was so random and so unexpected,

I crossed the street laughing. The power of the lies—*I am alone and no one cares about me*—was broken. And I couldn't wait to pack Jake's underwear, get to camp, and tell him what God had done for me.

Each time he helps me to extract a lie, a poisonous dart from Satan, God is faithful to comfort me and cure the wound, planting his healing love deeper into my heart. When I receive a special word from the Lord, not only do I believe the truth of his love automatically, but also my whole perspective changes. On the past: I forgive Jake, and I'm free from carrying a grudge. In the present: I feel the joy and energy of Jesus' company and I am able to communicate honestly with Jake. And for the future: there is always hope that God will continue to help me in this intimate way. This deeper sort of repentance—the *confession* of having believed lies, combined with *waiting* on God—brought healing to the long-held wounds of my heart, and subsequently to our marriage.

After our Healing for the Nations retreat furlough, we had returned to Bolivia for one more year so Caris could graduate from high school and Jake could turn over the camp ministry to the capable nationals. We had lived in Bolivia for twenty-one years, and though we felt sad about leaving, Jake and I were agreed (though our Bolivian friends were not) that it was time for us to go. In our minds, we were headed toward Spain, but before moving to Europe, we decided to take a leave of absence to renovate the ninety-year-old house we owned in North Carolina.

They say building a house is a guaranteed stressor on a marriage, with all the pressures of multiple decisions, differing tastes, and financial demands. But miraculously Jake and I rarely entered our old boxing ring. Through the discipling-my-own-heart tool, God revealed lies and deposited his healing love into my soul, helping Jake and I talk through each difference of opinion and settle each conflict. As Jake tore down our old house walls and built a beautiful new home, God dismantled the unhealthy patterns in our relationship and remodeled us. It was the finest season of our married life, and I thank God for the inner healing he began that year still continues.

We didn't know it then, but God was equipping us to live in remote Africa—not Spain. That's where my American neighbor would later call us "lovey-dovey." And it's where the battle against the darts and lies would become like a war.

8
~

A Trusting

*It's taken me my whole life to understand that
with God I do not have to understand.*
—MARY CROWLEY, *Think Mink*

A sweet wind of relief blew over me the moment Jake and I realized we were *not* going to move to Spain. We had completed our work in Bolivia and had been thinking of starting a camp in Spain, where our daughter Gaby and her husband lived. I had not been eager to live in Europe, but we thought God was leading that way. For two years, we expected something to open up—a property for sale or a team to join. Nothing concrete happened, so the day came when Jake and I both knew that Spain was not the next place for us.

God must have a great surprise ahead! Secretly I dreamed of hosting a retreat camp in North Carolina, our American home base—where we'd be close to our friends and our church, and where Caris, our youngest daughter, was attending college. So when some mission leaders asked Jake to go to Ethiopia, East Africa to oversee the development of a sports camp, I paid little attention. *What do we know about sports ministry? Jake could be a camp consultant for them, perhaps. He could travel back and forth and help them out. Maybe I could even travel over there with him a time or two. But surely God is not asking us to live there. I'm too old.*

I was 55. Funny how that seemed old at the time. How could I adjust to life in an African culture, put a new and difficult language into my head, and fit more people groups into my heart? Living and working in faraway Ethiopia was definitely *not* the great surprise I was imagining. A few months went by, and Jake continually believed God was offering us this opportunity. It would be the first ever residential camp in Ethiopia, an extension of an interdenominational soccer ministry involving hundreds of coaches and thousands of children all over the country. They wanted a place where their leaders could take their boys and spend quality time with them, giving them an experience of a lifetime, a week at a camp. I knew that Jake Wetzel was the right man for the challenge, but what about me? What would I do in Africa? What would happen to my dreams for a retreat ministry?

I remember standing in church one Sunday in August, salty self-pity leaking from my eyes as I looked around at all the familiar faces and moaned inwardly, *Why me, Jesus? Why couldn't some of these people go?* When I was a child at summer camp, I had pictured myself as a missionary in Africa—but that was then, and now was totally different. I did not want to go to Ethiopia.

On the following Saturday morning of that summer, I repeated my big questions to Jake. "What about me? How can you say this is God's will for us if God hasn't told *me*?"

Jake refused to fight back. "Sarah, like I've said all along, if God doesn't change your heart, we won't go," he said calmly.

"But how *long* are you going to wait for God to change me?" I spat back.

"Alright, okay," he told me. "I'll call on Monday and tell them we can't do it." And with that, he left for the hardware store.

I didn't want Jake to call the mission and back out. I knew that wasn't right. But why hadn't God given me a word, a reassurance? Why hadn't God done something to let me know he hadn't forgotten about me? I took my journal, our "Daily Light" book of Scripture, and my heavy frustration outside to the porch, and slumped down into an old plastic chair. I had tried reasoning (or rather, arguing) with Jake; now I would make my protest clear to God. I opened the book to that day's date and read these verses: "Don't be impatient. Wait for the Lord, and he will come and save you! . . . Fear not, for I am with you. Do not be dismayed, I am your God. I will strengthen you; I will help you" (Psalm 27:14; Isaiah 41:10, TLB).

I sensed God wanted me to remember these promises, that he would help me and strengthen me in Africa, but still my heart resisted. Then the next verse got me: "Those who still reject me are like the restless sea, which is never still, but always churns up mire and dirt. There is no peace, says my God, for them!" (Isaiah 57:20, TLB). The words described me exactly. Restless. Churned up. Without peace. But rejecting God? *Lord*, I said in my heart, *I know I am rejecting the idea of living in Africa, but how have I rejected you?*

Immediately, the words of Proverbs 3:5 came to me: "Trust in the Lord with all your heart and do not lean on your own understanding." It was such an old familiar verse, and like background music I had heard it quoted over and over that summer and had paid no attention. Sitting on the porch that morning, I realized I had been focused on trying to understand why God would ask me to go to Africa and it was clear I did not trust him. *You are right, Lord. By not trusting you, I am rejecting you. But God*, my heart cried, *I don't want to go to Ethiopia. What am I going to do there?*

In that instant, I "heard" two questions: *What if I give you a retreat ministry in Africa? What if I bring women to you, so you can share with them the healing I have given you?* I could never have imagined those questions on my own; I knew God had put those thoughts into my mind. A feeling of wonder came over me.

Wow. So that's your plan, Lord? A retreat ministry in Ethiopia? Not Spain. Not North Carolina. Wow. That's random. That's amazing. Okay. Wow. My hard heart melted, and by the time Jake returned from the hardware store, the restless sea in my soul had calmed. I knew God wanted us to go to Ethiopia; I trusted he had a good plan for me. And after a long walk and discussion with Jake, he, too, saw my change of heart and that night I slept peacefully.

The next day was a Sunday. Standing in church, I looked around at the same faces as the week before and tears filled my eyes again. This time, though, they were tears of awe. *Out of all these people, God, you are choosing me?* The words of Proverbs 3:5 had grabbed me for good. I don't have to understand; I just have to trust God.

My carefree joy about moving to Ethiopia was not to last, but the memory of that defining moment did. I never doubted that God wanted us in Africa.

Almost a full year later, in June of 2007, after twenty-five hours of traveling, we arrived in Addis Ababa, the sprawling capitol of Ethiopia. It was night; we could see black hills and dim lights of skyscrapers and winding roads. Those first days as we taxied around, doing the necessary paperwork in various parts of the city, we were all eyes. Tall, modern-looking buildings, many under construction. Corrugated tin roofs everywhere. A myriad of small stores. Green-covered hillsides off in the distance. Homes hidden behind high walls topped with barbed-wire or broken glass. Sidewalks lined with lean-to tents, their walls formed by plastic and swaths of old cloth. Super-sized orange buses, all sorts of trucks, Toyotas, and taxis, with each driver, as it says in Judges 21:25, doing "what was right in his own eyes." Everywhere there was rust and mud (it was rainy season), the pungent scent of Ethiopian *beriberi* spice, and the crush and flow of coffee-colored people—business-suited men, bands of cheeky street-boys, young people in jeans and t-shirts, and women draped in Muslim black or Orthodox white.

It was daunting to think this was our new home.

The first year was language school, and we tried our best to learn Amharic—to read, write, and pronounce the 240 Dr. Suess-like artsy letters of the alphabet. It was a mental challenge that gave me an ache in my head almost daily. And since for most of my adult life I had been a home-based mom, my own boss, enjoying my free mornings to exercise and do housework, it was a big task for me to be dressed nicely and out the door by eight o'clock each and every day.

Plus, the cultural differences pushed my emotions every time I walked around the city. Because of my white skin, I was stared at and followed wherever I went. Seeing the widespread poverty, the deprivation and suffering, hating the inequalities in the world, I carried the burdens of grief, anger, guilt, fear, and powerlessness. Having lived in Bolivia, one of the poorest countries in South America, I was perhaps a tad prepared to live in another developing country. Yet Africa felt heavier, and it hurt my heart.

The first years of cultural adjustments and language school are well-known among missionaries as a time of intense struggle for self-esteem. The enemy of my soul had an easy time accusing me, because I would often agree with him. *I don't belong here. I am stupid. I can't do this.* But whenever I took the time to sit down and pray through a lie and repent of believing it, God would deposit his truth deep inside, and I would get up and carry on. The day I finished language school, although I was exhausted, I jumped and danced around our apartment, singing praises to God. I couldn't speak Amharic well, but I felt hilariously victorious because both Jake and I had finished the course without quitting and without an emotional breakdown. I still rejoice for that miracle!

Then we moved to our assigned workplace, four hours south of Addis Ababa, at the SIM Langano Mission Station, where the sports camp was being developed. It's a beautiful property—eighty acres of forest along a scenic freshwater lake, far from phones and internet, electricity and stores. At that time, the station was a thoroughly hopping place, with a clinic that served a hundred patients a day, an elementary school with three hundred local Oromo children in grades K through 5, and a small evangelical church. These organizations were manned by three dedicated but overworked missionaries and at least thirty national employees:

guards, clinic workers, and teachers, most of whom lived on the mission compound property.

When we arrived, there was no place for us to live, so our first task was to fix up a small camper cabin for ourselves. Once we were settled, Jake began his work. In addition to renovating the existing kitchen and conference hall, there was site planning, designing and building new cabins, a bath house, and a chapel, keeping financial accounts, and encouraging camp leaders. All of this required the use of two African languages, and consulting three different supervisors for authorizations. It was a confusing and consuming project for Jake. But me? I didn't have a job. I didn't have a place. Besides fixing meals and washing dishes, clothes, and floors, I was free each day. Free to do whatever I found to do, but not free from fear. Discouraging thoughts dogged me. *I'm all alone. No one cares about me. They only wanted Jake. I don't matter.* The lies never stopped.

During the summer weeks when the camp program was in full swing, life was fulfilling. Sharing meals and prayer meetings and work with the young Ethiopian summer staff was a privilege, and watching those lanky, impoverished African kids laughing and playing and learning about Jesus was awesome. Camps were full and fun and the time went by fast, but that was only for eight weeks out of the year. The other weeks were long; each day seemed like two, and every hour dragged by. Although I tried, it was tough to keep the long view, to hang on to the big picture, the purpose of why we were there. Far from family, disconnected from the world, and having no specific role, I was often tempted to feel lazy, then ashamed, and then depressed.

In the past, I'd been a thriving Spanish-speaking missionary, a happy mom with a houseful of daughters, a content empty-nester enjoying her freedom, a woman with lots of friends. I loved talking about the gospel with people and leading small-group Bible studies. But during our first year at Langano, all of "me" seemed far away, and there was no way I could do the work I had previously enjoyed. I felt invisible. I felt useless. Who was I? And what did God want me to do? Everyone on the compound was busy. Was I only to be an observer, watching others live out their callings?

Eventually, Jake and I moved into our own made-from-a-shipping-container house under a huge sycamore fig tree on the edge of the camp section of the compound. As time went on, I got used to the fantastic myriad of bugs and the frequent and annoying visits by baboons that stole fruit off our screen porch and practiced gymnastics on our tin roof. Jake got rid of the bats (after a few nighttime battles and major improvements on the open eaves of our home—he's my hero!), and we were both entertained by the black-and-white colobus monkeys and the brilliant, plentiful birds. We got a phone, a dial-up internet connection, and a gas refrigerator. After two years, electricity was brought down the road. New missionaries arrived and friendships developed. Life became easier, but it was still isolated, lonely, and boring for me, and the battle against the lies continued.

I wondered, *God, what happened to that idea that I would have a retreat ministry to women in Langano?* I waited, but it seemed unlikely.

It was a gift I didn't really want—another daily devotional. I'd never heard of the author and I was turned off by the orange cover. But the giver of the gift was one of my favorite people in the world, a friend who is a missionary to Japan, so *Jesus Calling* went into my cases for Ethiopia. As soon as I started to read it, I was hooked. I read it each morning, and almost every time, Jesus had a word for me.

All I know about Sarah Young, the author of *Jesus Calling*, is what she wrote about herself in the introduction of the book. She was studying philosophy when her brother gave her Frances Schaeffer's *Escape from Reason*. That small book delighted her, and when she finished her master's degree she went to Europe to live and study at Schaeffer's school, L'Abri. It was there, one snowy, moonlit night in the mountains, that God first revealed his loving presence to her. "My involuntary response was to whisper, 'Sweet Jesus.' This utterance was totally uncharacteristic of me and I was shocked. . . . I realized it was the response of a converted heart: at that moment I knew I belonged to Him."[1] That began Sarah's intimate relationship with her Creator.

Over the next sixteen years, Sarah was occupied with earning a seminary master's degree in counseling and biblical studies, getting married, having two children, doing missionary church-planting work in Japan for eight years, then earning a second master's degree in counseling. About those years, Sarah writes, "I lived what many people might consider an exceptional Christian life. However, not once did I vividly experience the Presence of Jesus."[2]

During an unexpected lull in her busy life, while she and her husband were waiting for Australian visas so they could move to Melbourne to plant a Japanese church there, Sarah read Andrew Murray's book, *The Secret of the Abiding Presence.* She writes that what she learned from Murray was this: "God's Presence is meant to be the Christian's continual experience," and it's necessary to spend time alone with God "in quiet, uninterrupted communion."[3] Sarah began to seek God earnestly; every morning with Bible, pen, and paper, she listened to God.

Sarah Young's determination to listen to God resulted in many sweet experiences with Jesus. His presence strengthened her to deal with the lengthy, unexpected wait for overseas visas and with four surgeries for melanoma. In God's timing, they moved to Melbourne and Sarah began a counseling ministry for women. She soon realized that her experiences with God were not only for herself. From then on, her times alone with God were spent writing down what she heard. Many Christians long for a deeper experience of Jesus' presence; that is why Sarah published her writings. She says, "The Bible is, of course, the only inerrant word of God."[4] And all her devotionals—written as if Jesus were speaking the words—include Scripture fragments and guide the reader to God's word.

In rural Ethiopia, I desired a deeper experience of God's presence. I needed repeated assurances that God was with me, and that he would help me. God used the daily readings from Sarah Young's book and its major themes of thankfulness and trust to help me endure, one day at a time, one morning at a time.

On the metal wall of the white-painted shipping container that was my sweet little kitchen, I hung a bell-pull tapestry with the words from Proverbs 3:5: "Trust in the Lord with all your heart and do not lean on your own understanding." When the wind blew through our little house, that tapestry would flap and knock as if to say, "Look at me! Are you remembering these commands?" And *Jesus Calling* on my breakfast table reiterated the same. Every morning that I woke up with dread, each time I was anxious, grieved, or irritated, every time I was leaning on my own understanding, Jesus would grant me repentance and prove his love for me.

Even though life at Langano was a struggle, on the very first day of the very first camp, God did something to make sure I could trust him to help me. A visiting American surprised me with a valuable gift, a Baby Taylor guitar. She had brought it to give away, and try as I might, I could not convince her to give it to an Ethiopian. She insisted it was for me. That little guitar brought me a loud message of God's care—he knows I love to play the guitar—and undeserved grace—very undeserved, because on that day I was angry at him and with the mission for putting us there without providing a house for us. As I walked back to my cabin, with that precious gift slung over my shoulder, tears flowed from my eyes and I shook my head in amazement. God was affirming me—*Yes, I know this is going to be hard for you, Sarah*—and encouraging me—*Do not fear. I will help you sing your way through.*

Another early and undeserved blessing was being with the Ethiopian people: generous, hospitable, faith-filled, beautiful Ethiopian Christians. I was asked to interview leaders when they arrived at camp and find out how they became believers in Christ. I listened to their stories of faith, persecution, and miracles, then gathered them together into a booklet called *Transformed Lives* for others to read. What a privilege!

When I tried to draw the beautiful Ethiopian faces, I discovered I had more skill for art than I knew. I worked through two self-help drawing books and eventually printed a set of cards made from my pen and ink drawings—which I still sell for donations for the school and clinic.

Jesus said, "Whoever welcomes a little child like this in my name, welcomes me."
matthew 18:5

This is the first drawing of an Ethiopian girl that I made into a card. I call her "Welcome."

And when a pair of zebra-striped hoopoes walked past my screen porch one morning, I became addicted to birding. Those birds were fascinating: copious, colorful, and captivating. Their exotic whistles and unique warblings created a dramatic and constant musical score to Langano life; their variety of shapes, sizes, and sorts amazed everyone who took the time to look. I passed many hours observing birdlife. In fact, I identified over 200 species and self-published a children's coloring book, *The Incredible Birds of East Africa*. Like I said, God gave me unique gifts in Langano. While camp was empty for ten months of the year we'd settle into a kind of *Little House on the Prairie* life. Wearing a long skirt every day, playing cards by candlelight, working puzzles, game nights with other missionaries, cutting my own hair, using sponge rollers (My hair got healthy in Africa—that was a bonus!), swimming in the lake, eating homemade tortillas with fresh tilapia, making pizzas, cookies, and bread (with our starch-based diet, I gained fifteen pounds—that was an unwelcome bonus), washing our clothes in our tiny semi-automatic machine called Magic Queen (I loved her!), and wearing sweet-smelling, sundried clothes. There were many pleasures of that simple life.

Every morning after our eight o'clock devotions with the other missionaries, while the others rushed off to work, I walked the sandy loop around our compound, memorizing songs, Scriptures, or poetry, and enjoying the beauty around me. Year-round, there were balmy fragrant breezes, lovely clouds in high skies, spreading acacia thorn trees and grand old sycamores, the large sweetwater lake surrounded by distant blue mountains, and stunning varieties of sunsets and rainbows. Uncommon blossoms and birds—oversized and noisy ones, such as the fish eagles and hornbirds; florescent, miniature ones, such as the sunbirds and pigmy kingfishers—and bizarre bugs populated our "community." And on clear nights, the stars. Oh! the stars, like the birds, were abundant and stunning. It was a beautiful outdoor life.

During my second year there, God, through a counselor I sought out for help with my situational depression, gave me the idea to shadow my neighbors, the women missionaries who lived such busy lives on our compound. I talked with the ladies and we made a schedule. On Tuesdays, I went with the community health nurse to visit new babies or check on latrine use. Every Wednesday morning, I went to the clinic and stood by the young nurse practitioners as they did prenatal checkups. On Thursdays, I helped at the local school doing poster art, or just watching and smiling at the children as they watched and smiled at me. And on Fridays, I played arithmetic games and taught art for the homeschooled children to give their teacher a break. Like a momma, I felt proud of those gals and privileged to watch them do their work.

For a week, I drove the van for the clinic staff all around the area, across dusty roads, through corn fields and dry river beds, searching for families who had been served at the clinic to complete a survey. Once I watched the birth of a baby boy at the clinic. One dark midnight, I accompanied the nurse as she drove the clinic's Toyota, transporting the still-warm body of a mother who had died in childbirth to her family hut. These amazing experiences were also great gifts from God.

But even with all the gifts he gave me, I struggled. The days were long and physically, emotionally, and psychologically demanding. Like the Israelites in the wilderness, I knew God's very real help, but it was still the wilderness.

The greatest blessing of that time was Jesus himself. Through the devotional book *Jesus Calling*, I felt his nearness. He counseled me, he comforted me, and he helped me get out of my house over and over, with words such as these:

> Stop trying to work things out before their times have come. Accept the limitations of living one day at a time. When you follow this practice, there will be a beautiful simplicity about your life.[5]

> Draw near to Me with a thankful heart. Whenever you feel anxious remind yourself that your security rests in Me alone. You will never be in control of your life's circumstances but you can relax and trust in My control. Instead of striving for a predictable, safe lifestyle, seek to know Me in greater depth and breadth. I long to make your life a glorious adventure.[6]

Understanding will never bring you Peace, that is why I have instructed you to trust in Me, not in your own understanding. Human beings have a voracious appetite for trying to figure things out in order to gain a sense of mastery over their lives. But the world presents you with an endless series of problems. As soon as you master one set, another pops up to challenge you. The relief you had anticipated is short-lived. Soon your mind is gearing up again, searching for understanding (mastery) instead of seeking Me (your Master).[7]

The day came when our Langano time was over. I'm not going to lie; I was glad. My struggles with aloneness; the burden of filling up all my free time; the mental battles against lies; Jesus speaking, and the repeated sense of his peaceful presence; the hard, the bad, and the beautiful—it all ended in the winter of 2010. Despite the fact that God did not give me a specific ministry for women as I had imagined, even though I did not lead any women's retreats at Camp Langano, it was an unexpected, significant retreat for me. And I'm still reaping the rewards.

As I relate this chapter of my life, I'm tempted to feel ashamed. Many other women have truly difficult circumstances—like cancer or widowhood—and have persevered through far worse life situations than mine. As I write this, I am reading a book about an American family who starved for three-and-a-half years in a Japanese prison camp during World War II. Compared to so many, I am a wimp, a spoiled brat. Just like I did not deserve that Taylor guitar, I do not deserve God's favor.

But that is the very point. If God's grace, comfort, and strength came only to the deserving, which of us would be able to carry on? He helps us, no matter how often we fail or rebel, as long we keep returning to him, keep trying to trust him. Ethiopia was my wilderness, where my faith endurance was tried day by day. Jesus helped me through it, with great benediction. But I know there will be other life challenges ahead. And I pray that the truth of Proverbs 3:5 and the *Jesus Calling* lessons I embraced at Langano will never leave me: *I don't have to understand. I just have to follow close to Jesus, one day a time.* That's how I made it through nearly four years in Ethiopia, including one challenge I never could have anticipated.

I'll need a whole chapter to tell that story.

9
~

A Surrendering

I wish Thy way
But when in me myself would rise
And long for something otherwise
Then, Holy One, take sword and spear
And slay.

—AMY CARMICHAEL

It was late on a warm August African night in 2008. Our daughter Caris had come to visit us in Ethiopia on her summer break from college. Her presence was a great comfort and support to me while Jake and I transitioned from city life in Addis Ababa to remote life at Camp Langano. For our first month at camp, we three shared a one-room cabin named *Love*, and as we lay in our beds that August evening, Caris whispered, "Mom, I think I have feelings for Elias."

Elias was one of the Ethiopian camp staff—a soccer coach, gentle, handsome, and an excellent leader. We had worked with him the summer before, and we admired and respected him very much, as did everyone else at camp. Caris had jumped right in to all the camp activities and "coincidentally" was placed on Elias's small team for three out of the four weeks she was there. There was a thick language barrier between them, but at the end of the month, she let us know she was having "feelings."

My initial reaction was *Oh, NO!* Inwardly I gave myself a pep talk. *Okay. Stay calm, Sarah. She's about to go back to North Carolina. She'll forget this summer fling. Sure, Jake and I met at summer camp and were married six months later, but that's totally different. And oh, yeah, don't worry, Sarah, Elias is not a flirty guy like the other staff boys. He would never court an American girl. Nothing will come of this.* But a few days later, Caris left camp with a gift from Elias and a letter he'd instructed her to open on the plane.

Having studied at the language and orientation school for nine months, I'd heard stories about the fervent faith of Ethiopians and how God listens to and answers their prayers. The student who had sat next to me in class was a British girl—newly married to an Ethiopian man. From her, I had learned that Christian Ethiopians living in the urban centers have a distinctive way of "dating."

When a young man notices a girl and thinks he'd like to marry her, he first prays about her for a while. Next he asks her to pray with him about their future. If she says yes, they will be secretly connected by prayer for however long it takes until they become sure it is God's will to be married. At that point, they tell their pastor. Then the church elders plan a visit to the girl's family to ask for their blessing, and immediately the wedding planning begins. It's a long, slow process, but when Caris told me about the letter Elias had written to her—even though I had no idea what he'd said in it—in my mind, he was practically proposing marriage. I knew a serious young man like Elias would not approach a foreign girl unless he believed God was bringing them together.

My heart froze. There was no way I wanted my daughter to marry an African.

In a bookstore in the Dallas airport on one of my return trips to Ethiopia, I saw the fiftieth anniversary celebration display of *To Kill a Mockingbird*. On a whim, I bought a copy and took it with me. I found out later that the novel is one of the most popular books of all time, having sold an estimated forty million copies and translated into more than forty different languages. It was the only book Harper Lee ever wrote. I had read it years before, in one of my high school English classes. As I reread it while living in Africa, I was transported to the 1930s, to the small town of Maycomb, Alabama, to the people and the social problems of that day. And something happened to me as I read about them.

Caris and Elias sporadically wrote letters back and forth. During that time, I tried to talk her out of the friendship. Marriage is difficult, I would tell her, and how much harder it would be for them, with the language, cultural, economic, and educational differences they would face. My years in Ethiopia had been a wilderness challenge for me, and I didn't want Caris to suffer as I had. It was killing me that Caris kept saying she thought God was bringing them together. And it was killing her that her parents were not sharing her happiness.

This went on for two years. Caris moved slowly, patiently waiting for our blessing. We gave our permission for her to move forward, hoping that she would see the hard realities and run from them. Instead, the more she got to know Elias, the more she loved him.

We loved Elias too. By now we had worked with him for three summers; we knew his outstanding reputation, and we knew that he was not courting an American for a ticket to life in the United States. He was a calm, deep soul, acquainted with suffering. He knew and loved God. I recognized that he had the perfect complementary personality for our effervescent Caris. Still, my heart broke each time I thought about them together.

The main storyline of *To Kill a Mockingbird* follows lawyer Atticus Finch as he defends a black man named Tom, who is unjustly accused of raping a white girl. Atticus agrees to defend Tom, even though he predicts correctly that they will lose the case because of the all-white, prejudiced jury. Atticus' two children, Jem and Scout, witness the ongoing drama of that three-year period, with its public clashes between whites and blacks, rich and poor. They watch their father take a stand against the shameless townspeople, who are unduly mean to all black people. At the same time, Atticus will not allow Jem and Scout to condemn them. He is free from prejudice toward everyone. As I read the story of the turmoil of those days in American history, I realized that I, like Jem and Scout, was judging the judgmental townsfolk. *How can anyone be so blind?* I wondered.

Atticus told his brother Jack, "I hope and I pray that I can get Jem and Scout through this without bitterness, and most of all without catching Maycomb's usual disease. Why reasonable people go stark raving mad when anything involving a Negro comes up, I don't pretend to understand. . . . I just hope that Jem and Scout come to me for their answers instead of listening to the town. I hope they will trust me enough."[1]

Many of the adults in the southern state where I grew up displayed symptoms of that "Maycomb disease": prejudice, bitterness, fear. As a child, I breathed in the germs of that culture, but I thought I had escaped infection. Even if I had a little bit of the illness, surely I'd recovered during my years in college in the North. I was not prejudiced. *Was I?*

Atticus didn't have answers for me, but Jesus did. Atticus wanted his children to trust him for answers. I needed to trust Jesus.

At that time, I "happened" to be listening to a sermon series on the New Testament book of James, and the verses in chapter 2:1–6 hit me:

My brothers, show no partiality as you hold the faith in our Lord Jesus Christ. For if a man wearing a gold ring and fine clothing comes into your assembly, and a poor man in shabby clothing also comes in, and if you pay attention to the one who wears the fine clothing and say, "You sit here in a good place," while you say to the poor man, "You stand over there," or, "Sit down at my feet," have you not then made distinctions among yourselves and become judges with evil thoughts? Listen, my beloved brothers, has not God chosen those who are poor in the world to be rich in faith and heirs of the kingdom . . . ? But you have dishonored the poor man.

There it was. Clear words, finding me guilty. I realized that I do make distinctions and judgments about people according to race, education, or economic status. Unconsciously, I had been asking Elias to "stand over there," away from our family. God loved Elias and had chosen him to be rich in faith, and I was dishonoring both him and God. How ugly. With great sadness, I admitted my prejudice. I know God heard my confession, and I know he forgave me.

Yet the struggle in my heart continued. I was still unwilling to support Caris marrying an African. When she graduated from college, Caris moved from North Carolina to Addis Ababa, four hours away from us at Langano, to teach English for two months and to experience a real taste of life in Ethiopia. Elias was in her English class. One evening, she called down to camp and asked if they could come visit for the weekend. They wanted to "talk" with us. My stomach cramped up. "Not yet, please," I think is what I told her—although I probably didn't say please. "I can't handle this." We hung up abruptly, and I slept very little that night.

Early the next morning, on an exercise walk around the sandy camp road, I got severely honest with God. *Okay, God. I'm sorry I'm prejudiced.*

I know I'm wrong, and I want you to change my heart. But God, I don't want Caris to live in Africa! It will be too hard for her. I don't want her to suffer as I have here. I am the one who knows and loves her most in this world and I am against this. Lord, why is she not listening to me? Why is she insisting on her way? Why is she rebelling?

In my spirit, I heard these words: "Maybe *you* are the one who is rebelling."

*Auggh. Not me again. Why is it always **me** who has to repent?* My spirit groaned. *But, Lord, don't you see? I can't do this. I can't give my daughter to Africa.*

God's next words pierced me.

"I'm not asking you to give her to Africa. I'm asking you to give her to *me.*"

When I reached my cabin, I lay down on my bed and wept. God was right. God is always right. I was demanding my own way. I was rebelling against his will. With tears of surrender, my resistance dissolved and I fell into a deep, unusual sleep. When I woke up, I felt a profound serenity in the room and in my soul. The battle was over. God had won. I was the conquered one, yet also the victor, experiencing peace and rest.

From that morning on, I knew all would be well. My mind was so quickly, so totally changed, it boggled even me. I had no doubt that it was God's good plan for Caris to marry Elias. God would prosper her, and us too. I couldn't help smiling with an unexpected sense of anticipation. *What blessings does God have in store for me—for our whole family—through Elias and his rich faith?*

"It is a sin to kill a mockingbird," Harper Lee writes in her story.[2] Although the book is fiction and Atticus Finch is not a real person, God used this story to reveal my sin: self-righteousness, discrimination, racism, fear. I thought I had escaped the Maycomb disease, but my heart was sicker than I knew.

Worse than these sins in my heart was my attitude of rebellion against God. I wanted to have my way in Caris's life. I wanted to be God. How arrogant, how utterly foolish of me. How ashamed I feel recalling this. But it's true. And I know it's also true that "where sin increased, grace abounded all the more" (Romans 5:20). I did not deserve God's loving and miraculous intervention; I did not merit his forgiveness and peace.

That's the beauty of God's grace—it is for everyone, and there is nothing we can do to earn it. The only way we miss this grace is by cherishing our sin and refusing to go to Jesus. "Repent, therefore, and turn again, that your sins may be blotted out, that times of refreshing may come from the presence of the Lord" (Acts 3:19, 20). Repentance is a great gift from God. Every time I recognize and confess my wrong actions or thoughts, my sins are "blotted out"—even the grave sin of rebelling against God! And I experience the special refreshment that comes from his presence. It's all grace!

Caris and Elias did come to visit us at camp that weekend, two years after she'd first whispered to me her feelings for him, two years of my hoping her feelings would change. Both Jake and I enjoyed watching them stroll about camp and play games together, listening to their stories and their dreams. Six months later, Caris and Elias were formally engaged. Wholeheartedly I cheered them on, helping with all the planning and details as they "marched forth" to March 4th, 2012, their wedding day.

Caris and Elias forged a beautiful relationship. They weathered the cultural differences and grew strong serving the Lord together. They had lots of handsome sons. When they were older, Elias became the prime minister of Ethiopia and Caris made a wonderful first lady. Please note: These last three sentences were facetiously dictated to me by Caris as she reviewed this chapter to offer feedback. She has since decided she does not want Elias to be prime minister. In reality, she and Elias are happy newlyweds, living in the same little house Jake and I lived in, dealing with the same bugs and baboons, flourishing in their work at Camp Langano, maneuvering the ups and downs of life in Africa better than her parents did.

I'm deeply grateful for their happiness. And for my own! God orchestrated all those details to show me how blind I was, how wrong I was. He guided my steps to the bookshop table and led me to pick up *To Kill a Mockingbird*. He provided the teaching tapes on James. And I'll never forget the miraculous conversation on that sandy Ethiopian road and the other-worldly peace he placed in my heart after I had wept on my bed. This is a story of God's patience and gentleness, of his great mercy and undeserved grace.

It was the longest active rebellion I ever waged against God—two years! But it wouldn't be the last time I would try to refuse what God was doing in my life. The challenge of submitting to God's will continues.

10
~

An Accepting

This life therefore is not righteousness but growth
in righteousness. Not health but healing;
not being but becoming; not rest, but exercise. We are not
yet what we shall be, but we are growing toward it.
The process is not yet finished, but it is going on,
this is not the end, but it is the road. All does not yet
gleam in glory, but all is being purified.
—MARTIN LUTHER[1]

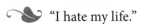 "I hate my life."

I wrote those words in my journal on a July morning just two years ago. No matter that I was sitting on a hillside above the whitewashed, red-tiled, flowered city of Granada in Spain; the beautiful view of the snowy Sierra Nevada mountains was lost on me. My sights were on myself, because my heart was heavy. In the dark, wee hours of that day, I had watched my daughter Johannah leave on a bus bound for Madrid to catch a flight to Vancouver, Canada, where she lives. Johannah and I had met in Granada to await the birth of Rebeca, my daughter Gaby's first child.

113

Sharing a tiny, hot office-*cum*-guestroom for two weeks, I rebonded with Joh. I really like her and I miss her when we're apart. For the record, I really-really-really-really like *all* four of our girls, but on that particular day, it was Johannah I was pining for. I was thinking about the long trip before her, wishing we could be together more, and I was dreading what was to come. A few days later it would be my turn to leave Gaby and her newborn and fly back to North Carolina. These fresh good-byes would be added to my collection of farewells I'd experienced over the years of missionary living. That morning on the lonely mountainside, the well-known heavy rock sank in my gut, and a familiar growing lump choked my throat. Dread spewed out onto my journal with those words: *I hate my life.*

Jake and I have four daughters. They each live on a different continent, in a different country. Canada. United Arab Emirates. Spain. Ethiopia.

Johannah works at a Christian university and church in the inner city of Vancouver, British Columbia, Canada. Miah is an art teacher; both she and her husband teach at an American school in the United Arab Emirates. Gaby and her Brazilian husband are settled in Granada, Spain, where they're missionaries in a new church plant. And Caris, at that time, was engaged to marry an Ethiopian man, with plans to live and work in sports camp ministry in his east African country. Not one daughter lives in my country, the United States. Now according to me, this is not how life is supposed to be.

While I was 4,000 miles away from home there in Spain, my Dubai daughter, Miah, and her family, were vacationing in North Carolina with Jake. I was totally missing out on seeing my two-year-old granddaughter, Harper, which meant I would never see Harper as a two-year-old. I was sitting on that huge disappointment. I was also thinking about Caris, who was scheduled to depart the next month for language school and her new life in Ethiopia. Each time a good-bye loomed, I felt that visceral rock and lump, like impending death, and I was weary of this emotional "dying."

Nursing my hurt and disappointment, I realized I was very angry. (I have learned that disappointment is often a cover word for anger.) Yes, I was angry with God. He had denied my request that Rebeca be born on time, hence denying me that visit with my Dubai daughter and grand-daughter. And it seemed he was continually denying me a shared life with any of my daughters. *How can I live with God's denials?* I demanded. Even though I knew the old saying was true—"In acceptance lies peace"—I couldn't force myself to accept what I hated.

All those thoughts were stomping around my head that morning, when I sat down on a rock and opened my Bible to read about Josiah in 2 Chronicles 34 and 35. The first part of the story was familiar, a favorite Bible story of mine, about the boy-king Josiah who "did what was right in the eyes of the Lord" (2 Chronicles 34:2). But the rest of his story was new to me.

Josiah was only eight years old when he became king of Judah. He was sixteen when he began to seek the God of David, and by age twenty he had set out to purge his kingdom and the city of Jerusalem of its pagan idols and altars to Asherim and Baal. When King Josiah was in his mid-twenties, he strongly supported the high priest Hilkiah in repairing and restoring the temple of the Lord. An old scroll of the Book of the Law was found and when his secretary, Shaphan, read it to him, Josiah ripped his clothes and grieved. His heart was broken, recognizing his people's long disobedience to God. He wanted everyone to know about the Lord's will. He called together all the people in the land for a public reading of the Law and led them in corporate repentance and returning to God.

When it came time for the Passover feast, Josiah commanded that everyone observe the feast according to every detail that was in the Law. Scripture tells us, "No Passover like it had been kept in Israel since the days of Samuel the prophet" (2 Chronicles 35:18). Josiah was serious about obeying God. But one time he failed and the consequence was severe.

Second Chronicles 35 records the story of Pharoah Neco of Egypt leading his army through the land of Judah, heading to a battle against the Babylonians. For some reason, King Josiah took his men and marched out to stop him. Neco sent him a message: "What have we to do with each other, king of Judah? I am not coming against you this day, but against the house with which I am at war. And God has commanded me to hurry. Cease opposing God . . . lest he destroy you" (v. 21).

I finished reading the story incredulously. Josiah "did not listen to the words of Neco from the mouth of God" (v. 22). That seemed un-Josiah-like. Why did he ignore God's message? Perhaps he rejected it because of who the messenger was, Neco, the leader of a pagan nation. But for whatever reason, Josiah disregarded the warning, disguised himself, and went into battle. Sadly, he was fatally wounded by the Egyptian archers when he was only thirty-nine years old. God's prediction through Neco came true.

I suppose God is accustomed to people ignoring his warnings, opposing him, rebelling against his will. It's been going on since the Garden of Eden. How arrogant we are. How foolish. Why do we think we can oppose God and live?

That morning I saw that *I* was opposing God. I was fighting against him because I didn't like what he was doing. I didn't like our Wetzel family reality. My anger and self-pity were not just surface sins, but actually the signs of rebellion, a defiant shaking-of-my-fist against God. Through Josiah's story, God warned me. The "COG" message was clear: *Cease Opposing God.* I had the choice—stop opposing his will, or continue to die emotionally with anger and bitterness.

A few weeks later, back home in North Carolina, a package arrived in the mail. A friend sent me Catherine Marshall's book *Light in My Darkest Night.* I had read many of her books in the past and always appreciated her honesty and spiritual wisdom, so I welcomed this one, even though I wasn't expecting it and had never heard of it before. As soon as I opened the cover, I was drawn in to the story about Catherine's greatest struggle for acceptance of God's will.

Catherine Marshall (1913–1983) wrote over thirty books. She was the wife of the well-known Presbyterian minister and United States Senate Chaplain Peter Marshall, who died young, leaving Catherine to raise their nine-year-old son, Peter John. Catherine's best-known works include *A Man Called Peter*, a biography of her husband, which was made into a movie, and the novel *Christy*, a fictionalized account of her mother's life as a teacher in impoverished Appalachia, which was also made into a movie as well as a TV series.

Catherine married Leonard LeSourd, an editor of *Guideposts Magazine*, in 1959. Five years after her death, using her journals and interviewing her friends, Leonard put together the book *Light in My Darkest Night*. It's the story of six agonizing months in her life, a time when she felt God removed his presence from her.

The death of her newborn grandchild was the event that pushed Catherine into the darkness. The baby, Amy Catherine, was born with a genetic abnormality and the family was told she would not live. Catherine felt the Lord leading her to fast and pray for the baby, and that he would heal her. With tremendous faith, she invited her closest friends to join her for a ten-day fasting retreat. She fully believed God would move in answer to their petitions and miraculously reverse the doctors' prediction. Every day at the hospital, two of the friends sat by the baby's incubator praying, while the rest of the party remained back at their seaside manor retreat, beseeching God for the miracle. As they prayed, little Amy did improve; but three weeks afterward, she died.

Catherine's sorrow over her granddaughter's death scrambled with the pain of confusion and betrayal. Why hadn't God done what he had promised he would do? Why had he dismissed their fervent prayers?

Why didn't he heal the baby? Grief and unanswered questions took over and Catherine withdrew from life, totally disheartened, unable to sleep or read or pray. God seemed absent to her, and she had no spirit to seek him.

After six months of solitude and soul-searching, Catherine wrote this:

> Do I have spiritual pride and is my dark night experience His way of chastening me? . . . I have never had a problem facing up to the fact that I am a sinner. Glibly I repeat, "I am a sinner saved by grace." By saying this, however, I place myself in a general category of sinners, enabling me to avoid facing up to the fact that I have committed, am committing, specific sins. . . . Then it hit me like a sledge-hammer blow. I am in rebellion against God.[2]

Catherine confessed her sin of rebellion, and also her self-pity, but still she did not have peace. One day a friend said to her, "Catherine, maybe it's your insistence on understanding that's the problem." Then God opened her eyes. In her words:

> Suddenly I was overwhelmed with remorse, embarrassment, gratitude, and relief, all mingled together as I saw . . . [that] for reasons of His own, God had allowed Amy Catherine to be born genetically damaged. Her death served God's purposes, fulfilled His plan in some specific way not revealed to us, just as Christ's death on the cross at first baffled and dismayed His disciples, but did not destroy their faith. What is destroying me is that I don't understand. I, from my tiny human vantage point demanding to see into the secrets of eternity![3]

Catherine finally realized that "understanding" was the key word in her difficulties. Since she had not understood why God allowed the baby to die, she had sulked and wallowed in misery for six months. But he granted her repentance. She wept, asking God to forgive her rebellion. She realized God had not turned away from her; her own sin had made her turn her back to God. God showed her the root of her rebellion, presumption. In her fervent prayers for Amy Catherine, she had been telling God what he was going to do; she had tried to be God in the baby's life. "Appalled, I tried to detach myself from this sin," she wrote. "There was no detachment. I had tried to usurp the power of the almighty God. 'O Lord, can You forgive me for this abomination?'"[4]

God did. The silence was broken and Catherine again felt the good fortune of God's merciful presence. She found peace and satisfaction in him, while relinquishing her need for understanding. God restored her soul.

Up on the mountain that day in Spain, in my spirit I felt God ask me, "Sarah, haven't you grieved long and hard enough about not being able to live near your children? Isn't it time you stop rebelling against my will for your family?" All I could do was bow my head. "Yes, Lord. You are right. Please forgive me."

I packed up my Bible and journal and followed the dusty road downhill, back to my daughter's neighborhood, back to the tiny, hot apartment, back to my life of repeated good-byes. One part of me was sighing. I had been exposed again, a sinner found out. But another part of me was singing. I felt a lively harmony of hope and curiosity in my soul, and I wondered how this newest application of God's lovingkindness and grace would change my heart.

I was soon to find out. A few days later, while packing my bags to leave my daughter Gaby and two-week-old Rebeca, I was uncharacteristically serene inside and out. Wow. That was certainly different! Usually I "pre-grieved" for days, carrying that rock of sorrow in my stomach before the looming good-bye. I would wistfully notice every "last" thing, such as "This is our *last* time to go to church together," or "This is our *last* breakfast," or "This is our *last* walk." I would try to appear calm and controlled, while the painful emotions of loss and anger churned inside, yanking me around and stealing my peace. When the good-bye finally came, I was often spent and numb, just wanting to get it over with, and then the whole next week I was weepy with the memories, thinking *This time last week, we were* _____. What torture I would put myself through! But no more. I left Spain feeling free.

Three weeks later, Jake and I put daughter Caris on the plane for her new life in Africa. I was surprised again. There had been brief sad moments, but I actually experienced joy helping her get ready to leave us. No hardrock pain in the gut. No strangling dread. God had done a heart-changing miracle for me—again.

In our North Carolina home, a quartet of clocks hang above the sliding glass door—four clocks set to four time zones, each with a city sign below: Vancouver. Granada. Langano. Dubai. The clock faces help me feel connected to my daughters; their cadenced tick-tick-tocking somehow comforts me and makes me smile.

I am proud of how our daughters are blossoming in the exotic corners of the world where God has placed them. And I'm proud that, although I will always miss them and will probably always bemoan the international travel, I, too, am thriving here in my spot. And oh, I am so very grateful! I love to tell the stories of God's provision and goodness to our family, or of accumulating the happy photos and experiences of repeated welcomes and noisy reunions in various places around the world. What a life.

That is not to say I have arrived and struggle no more. Hardly. The "cease opposing God" message given to me on that dry Spanish hillside continually applies. My heart naturally defaults to wanting my own way. But perhaps with all this practice, I'm getting quicker at repenting and believing that, in spite of myself, God always has grace for me.

What he did for Catherine Marshall—and for Isobel Kuhn, Keith Green, Jack Miller, Joni Eareckson Tada, Ken Moynagh, Roy Hession, Steve and Rujon Morrison, and Sarah Young—he will do for me. As he promises in Psalm 138:8, "The Lord will fulfill his purpose for me."

It's a journey. And because of Jesus, it's a good one. God keeps me growing down. Repenting and rejoicing. And I can wholeheartedly say: I love my life.

One Last Word

Remember the story in the New Testament about Zacchaeus? If you went to Sunday school like I did, you can probably sing his song: "Zacchaeus (Was a Wee Little Man)."[1] It's a popular Bible story for children but it's not for kids alone. I have heard it said that God grants freedom to man, even the freedom to reject his love. Zacchaeus's story is an important one, as it exemplifies our freedom and how repentance and acceptance of God's love go hand in hand.

Zacchaeus was a wealthy tax collector who lived in the city of Jericho. He was well-known, but not popular; everyone knew he was rich because he collaborated with the occupying Roman government and padded his own purse by overcharging his neighbors and kin.

One day the buzz around town was that Jesus was coming. Zacchaeus went out to the main road, "seeking to see who Jesus was" (Luke 19:3). But as you may know from the song, he was very short, so he scrambled up a tree to get the best view. That is the memorable part of the story: A short little man climbs a tree to see Jesus. But what did Zacchaeus see?

Jesus was walking down the dusty road, surrounded and jostled by his followers—men, women, and children, as well as demanding beggars and people pressing near him to be healed. At the precise moment, he ignored the noisy crowd, stopping to look up at Zacchaeus, who was sitting on a branch of a sycamore tree. I imagine everyone else's eyes turning upward, too. A grown man perched in a tree. Precarious. Humorous. Undignified. At that moment, I think Jesus gave Zacchaeus his singular smile and a lot of honor when he said, "Zacchaeus, hurry and come down, for I must stay at your house today" (Luke 19:5). Jesus' face was turned to Zacchaeus with an undeniable look of love. That's what Zacchaeus saw.

Jesus knew Zacchaeus's name. He knew his profession. He knew his reputation. He knew his selfish and hurtful ways. Still he looked for him. He smiled at him. He wanted to be with him.

Now Zacchaeus had the freedom to say "No, thank you." He could have stayed where he was, in the tree, and in his life. He could have kept on collecting taxes, taking care of himself, amassing his own fortune. But he didn't. In the face of Jesus, he saw love. Acceptance. Grace, in spite of his sins. And he wanted to change. The Bible says Zacchaeus hurried down and received Jesus "joyfully" (verse 6) into his home and into his life. He repented of his wrongdoing, and his change of heart was evident by his public announcement to give money to the poor and recompense those he had cheated. Zacchaeus was never the same again.

You can read the whole story in Luke 19.

The greatest miracle is the miracle of a changed heart. That's what Jesus did for Zacchaeus that day because he did not reject God's offered grace. That's what Jesus does for me over and over: changes my heart by his grace. And he wants to do the same for you.

Jesus sees us wherever we are. He knows everything about us. And he always gives us grace in spite of ourselves. So, dear reader, as you close this book, I hope you will look at Jesus, accept his love, and follow him as Zacchaeus did, repenting and rejoicing. And thereby you will "grow in the grace and knowledge of our Lord and Savior Jesus Christ. To him be the glory both now and to the day of eternity. Amen" (2 Peter 3:18).

Newlyweds Jake and Sarah at Honey Rock Camp, Northwoods Campus of Wheaton College, Three Lakes, Wisconsin, 1974.

1987 Wetzel family prayer card, returning to Bolivia for second term.

Jake and Sarah in the Camp Kewiña kitchen, Bolivia, 1996.

Wetzel family at Camp Kewiña in 1997, not long before first daughter
Johannah left for college.

Sarah with campers at Camp Langano, Ethiopia, 2007.

The sweet little container house where Jake and Sarah lived for two-and-a-half years. Now it's "home sweet home" for Caris and Elias.

Sarah, Elias, Caris, Johannah, and Jake, at our Ethiopian wedding, 2012.

Family reunion in Montreat, North Carolina, 2012. Everyone but Elias was there.

Acknowledgments

Writing is solitary work. It took hours of confinement for me to get this book born. At the same time, the making of a book is a group effort and I am very grateful to God for the people who helped me fulfill my dream.

First of all, I thank God for *mis queridas hijas,* Johannah, Miah, Gaby, and Caris. Thank you, girls, for your love and encouragement, for enriching my life and always giving me grace. Johannah, thank you for reading my manuscript and offering sage and insightful advice. Thank you all for letting me tell our stories (especially you, Caris.) and thank you for bringing into our family three brilliant young men and four extraordinary grand-girls. It is for you and your children and their future cousins that I wrote this book.

Thank you, God, for my little sister. Mary, I valued your advice and editorial service; your opinions affirmed and boosted me more than you can know. And thank you, God, for my special cheerleading friends: Fran, Jessie, Chel, Clare, Sarah, Patsi, Francie, Jenni, Kathy, and others. When I was disheartened, just jotting you an email lifted my spirits. Thank you, sweet ladies.

Thank you, God, for my pastor, Richard White. Richard, I appreciate your examining my writing for theological truth. Thank you for preaching grace at Christ Community Church, for always pointing us to Jesus with your inspiring sermons and your humble life.

Dear God, I join thousands of people who thank you for Ken and Joni Eareckson Tada. Joni, thank you for offering to help me, and for giving me and my readers a great gift with your foreword. Most of all, thank you and Ken for living your lives as an open book and showing the world the powerful difference Jesus makes in a life.

Thank you, God, for connecting me to Deep River Books and for giving me Kit Tosello as my editor. Thank you, Kit, for your skills, enthusiasm, gentle editing, and excellent coaching. This book would not be what it is without you. I am deeply grateful to you.

I thank you, God, last of all, for giving me my dear husband, Jake, and "growing us down" together for forty years. Jake, thank you for all your help and understanding, especially these last two years as I have been distracted in this project. Thank you for riding your bicycle across America, inspiring me by your perseverance. For the rest of our lives, we will treasure the memories made those weeks you cycled the back roads across Wyoming, Montana, Idaho, and Washington while I pecked away on this book in small-town libraries and coffee shops. God has been so good to us. To him goes all the praise, honor, and thanks.

Notes

Foreword by Joni Eareckson Tada

1. Arthur Bennett, ed., *Valley of Vision, A Collection of Puritan Prayers* (Banner of Truth, 1975), xxiv.

Introduction

1. J. I. Packer, *Rediscovering Holiness: Know the Fullness of Life with God* (Ventura, CA: Regal, 2009), 109.

Chapter 1: A Yearning

1. Isobel Kuhn, *By Searching* (Chicago, IL: Moody Press, 1959), 13.
2. Ibid., 15.
3. Ibid., 16.
4. Kuhn, *In the Arena* (London, Great Britain: China Inland Mission, 1959), 14.
5. Ibid., 26.
6. Ibid., 40.
7. Ibid., 43.
8. Ibid., 40.

Chapter 2: A Disconnect

1. Melody Green and David Hazard, *No Compromise: The Life Story of Keith Green* (Chatsworth, CA: A Sparrow Press Book, 1989), 36.
2. Ibid., 38.

3. The biblical word *gospel* literally means "good news" and it refers to the Christian truths in the Bible, specifically this: God loves everyone, and whoever accepts his son Jesus as their Lord and Master is accepted by God.

Here's the problem: we are all self-focused. We like our independence. We want to run our own lives. We don't want God to rule over us. This is the definition of sin. Sin is not just our outward actions (lying, stealing, cheating, etc.); it is the whole inward bent of our hearts. We want our own way, not God's. We want to be in control.

The only way we can have acceptance with God, forgiveness, freedom from fear, guilt, and shame, and receive the gift of eternal life in heaven is to admit our selfish bent and turn from our controlling ways to Jesus. We must believe that his historical, sacrificial death on the cross proved his amazing love, took the punishment we deserve, and makes us fit for heaven. It is all by grace; there is nothing we can do to earn God's love. There is nothing we can do to deserve heaven. And when we accept his grace and commit ourselves to follow Jesus, to read and obey his Word in the Bible, he gives us joy, freedom, and power to live our lives—whatever comes. He is a good master. This gospel really is good news.

Chapter 3: A Humbling

1. These stories are taken from World Harvest Sonship lectures.
2. Ibid.
3. Ibid.
4. C. John Miller, *Repentance: A Daring Call to Real Surrender* (Fort Washington: PA: CLC Publications, 2009), 42.
5. Sonship lecture.

Chapter 4: A Flourishing

1. Patricia St. John, *Man of Two Worlds* (Worthing: Henry E. Walter Ltd., 1976), 27.

2. Ibid., 29.

3. Ibid., 30.

4. Ibid., 30.

5. Ibid., 31.

6. Ibid., 40.

7. Ibid., 43.

8. Ibid., 95.

9. Ibid., 96.

Chapter 5: A Suffering

1. Joni Eareckson Tada, *The God I Love* (Grand Rapids, MI: Zondervan, 2003), 218.

2. Tada, *Diamonds in the Dust* (Grand Rapids, MI: Zondervan Publishing House, 1993), Jan 14.

3. Ibid., Mar 10.

4. Ibid., Aug 2.

5. Ibid., Mar 14.

6. Ibid., Oct 28.

7. Ibid., Oct 17.

8. Ibid., Jan 31.

Chapter 6: A New Seeing

1. Roy Hession, *The Calvary Road* (London, Great Britain: Christian Literature Crusade, 1950), 13-14.

2. Ibid., 15.

3. Roy Hession, *My Calvary Road* (Grand Rapids, MI: Zondervan, 1978), 86.

4. Roy Hession, *We Would See Jesus* (Fort Washington, PA: Christian Literature Crusade,1958), 27.

5. Ibid., 30.

6. These are Hession's chapter titles in *We Would See Jesus*: "Jesus as All We Need," "Jesus as the Truth," "Jesus as the Door," "Jesus as the Way," and "Jesus as the End."

7. Roy Hession, *Good News for Bad People* (Fort Washington, PA: Christian Literature Crusade, 1990), 18-19.

8. Hession, *We Would See Jesus*, 44-45.

9. This promise is found in Romans 8:28: "We know that for those who love God he works all things together for good." In other words, God works in all things for the good of those who love him.

Chapter 7: A Healing

1. These quotes are taken from lectures at Healing for the Nations. www.healingforthenations.org.

2. Ibid.

Chapter 8: A Trusting

1. Sarah Young, *Jesus Calling* (Nashville, TN: Thomas Nelson, 2004), vii.

2. Ibid., viii.

3. Ibid., ix.

4. Ibid., xii.

5. Ibid., Mar 29.

6. Ibid., July 5.

7. Ibid., Aug 7.

Chapter 9: A Surrendering

1. Harper Lee, *To Kill a Mockingbird* (New York, NY: HarperCollins, 1960), 100-101.

2. Ibid., 103

Chapter 10: An Accepting

1. Martin Luther, "Defense of All the Articles," Lazareth transl., as found in Grace Brame, *Receptive Prayer* (Chalice Press, 1985), 119.

2. Catherine Marshall, *Light in My Darkest Night* (Grand Rapids, MI: Fleming H. Revell, 1989), 196.

3. Ibid., 201.

4. Ibid., 204.

One Last Word

1. Copyright unknown.

Bibliography

Green, Melody and David Hazard. *No Compromise: The Life Story of Keith Green*. Nashville, TN: Thomas Nelson, 2008.

Hession, Roy. *The Calvary Road*. London, Great Britain: Christian Literature Crusade, 1958.

Hession, Roy. *Good News for Bad People*. Fort Washington, PA: Christian Literature Crusade, 1990.

Hession, Roy. *We Would See Jesus*. Fort Washington, PA: Christian Literature Crusade, 1958.

Kuhn, Isobel. *By Searching*. Chicago, IL: Moody Press, 1959.

Kuhn, Isobel. *In the Arena*. London, Great Britain: China Inland Mission, 1959.

Lee, Harper. *To Kill a Mockingbird*. New York, NY: HarperCollins, 1960.

Marshall, Catherine. *Light in My Darkest Night*. Grand Rapids, MI: Fleming H. Revell, 1989.

Miller, C. John. *Repentance: A Daring Call to Real Surrender.* Fort Washington: PA: CLC Publications, 2009.

Morrison, Steve and Rujon. www.healingforthenations.org.

Packer, J. I. *Rediscovering Holiness: Know the Fullness of Life with God.* Ventura, CA: Regal, 2009.

St. John, Patricia. *Man of Two Worlds.* Worthing, Great Britain: Henry E. Walter Ltd., 1976.

Tada, Joni Eareckson. *Diamonds in the Dust.* Grand Rapids, MI: Zondervan Publishing House, 1993.

Young, Sarah. *Jesus Calling.* Nashville, TN: Thomas Nelson, 2004.

Contact the author:

growingdown.wetzel@gmail.com